PREVENTING
CHILD SEXUAL ABUSE

PREVENTING CHILD SEXUAL ABUSE

A Curriculum for Children
Ages Nine Through Twelve

Kathryn Goering Reid
with Marie M. Fortune

United Church Press

Cleveland

DEDICATION

For all children, including my own children, Derek, Jacob,
Mary, and Jesse, in hopes that they will grow up knowing that every
child is a child of God and every child is special.

Copyright © 1989, 2002 United Church Press
700 Prospect Avenue, Cleveland, Ohio 44115
unitedchurchpress.com

Scripture quotations designated **RSV** are from the Revised Standard Version of the Bible, copyrighted 1946, 1952, © 1971, 1973 by the Division of Christian Education of the National Council of Churches of Christ in the U.S.A., and are used by permission. In some instances adaptations have been made for the sake of inclusive language and for *clarity*. Scripture quotations designated **I-LL** are from *An Inclusive-Language Lectionary for Years A, B, and C,* copyrighted © 1983, 1984, and 1985, by the Division of Education and Ministry, National Council of Churches of Christ in the U.S.A., and used by permission. Scripture quotations designated **TEV,** are from the *Good News Bible: The Bible in Today's English Version;* Old Testament © American Bible Society in 1976; New Testament © American Bible Society 1966, 1971, and 1976, and used by permission.

Illustrator: Tom Novak

Library of Congress Cataloging-in-Publication Data

Reid, Kathryn Goering.
    Preventing child sexual abuse: a curriculum for children ages
nine through twelve / Kathryn Goering Reid, with Marie M. Fortune.

    Bibliography: p. 123, 124, 125, 126
    ISBN 0-8298-0810-8
    1. Child molesting—Prevention—Study and teaching (Secondary)—
United States.   2. Child molesting—Religious aspects—
Christianity.   3. Christian education of children—United States—
Curricula.   I. Fortune, Marie M.   II. Title.
HQ72.U53R45   1989
362.7'6—dc20   89-33084

United Church Press, 475 Riverside Drive, New York, New York 10115

Contents

Acknowledgments

This project would have been impossible without the support, care, and vision of the women at the Center for the Prevention of Sexual and Domestic Violence in Seattle, Washington: Marie Fortune, Frances Wood, and Jean Anton. Their enthusiasm and concern kept this project progressing.

In addition, the Advisory Board of the project gave guidance, feedback, and suggestions. Their patience and hard work helped bring all the different parts of this curriculum together. The Advisory Board was made up of the following clergy and lay people, who showed their concern for both the children of this society and the church: the Rev. Valerie DeMarinis, Assistant Professor of Pastoral Psychology, Pacific School of Religion, Reformed Church in America Minister; the Rev. Marie Fortune, United Church of Christ Minister, Center for the Prevention of Domestic and Sexual Violence; Jennie Winsor Payne, Religious Educator, United Church of Christ; the Rev. Elizabeth Oettinger, United Church of Christ Minister; Mary Schau, M.Ed., Religious Education, Roman Catholic; the Rev. Donna Di Sciullo, Unitarian Universalist Minister; Frances Wood, Center for the Prevention of Domestic and Sexual Violence; and the Rev. Suzanne K. Yates, Diaconal Minister, Christian Education, United Methodist Church. Suzanne Yates was especially helpful in presenting this material for testing. We express our gratitude to them for their hard work.

Much appreciation goes to the people who read through the curriculum, giving us important feedback and suggestions: the Rev. Thelma Burgonia-Watson, North Seattle Presbytery; Faith A. Johnson, United Church Board for Homeland Ministries; Alice Ray-Keil, Committee for Children, Seattle, Washington; and Gayle M. Stringer, Education Coordinator, King County Rape Relief, Renton, Washington.

Special thanks to the children of Epworth United Methodist Church, Berkeley, California. Epworth is a church that cares deeply about children and believes that they are special to us and to God. Both the adults and children of Epworth gave me a chance to test this material as well as encouragment and support throughout this project.

Most importantly, the encouragement and help from Dr. Stephen B. Reid, my husband, has been essential. He helps me struggle with issues of justice and theology. But most of all, he believes that the work that I do is important.

We gratefully acknowledge the generosity of the following supporters of this project:

Christian Church (Disciples of Christ)
General Reconciliation Committee
Indianapolis, Indiana

Church Women United
New York, New York

Epiphany Parish of Seattle
Seattle, Washington

Episcopal Church Center
Coalition for Human Needs
New York, New York

Fellowship of the Least Coin Fund
Multan, Pakistan

Forest Foundation
Tacoma, Washington

Ms. Foundation for Women, Inc.
New York, New York

Plymouth Congregational Church
Seattle, Washington

Presbyterian Church (U.S.A.)
Synod of Alaska/Northwest
Social Concerns Division
Seattle, Washington

Prince of Peace Lutheran Church
Seattle, Washington

Sister Mary Raymund O'Leary Mercy
Farmington Hills, Michigan

Sisters of Charity of Our Lady Mother of Mercy
East Haven, Connecticut

The L.J. Skaggs and Mary C. Skaggs Foundation
Oakland, California

United Church of Christ
United Church Board for Homeland Ministries
New York, New York

The United Methodist Church
General Board of Global Ministries
New York, New York

University Congregational Church
Seattle, Washington

Wyman Youth Trust
Seattle, Washington

Preface

The Center for the Prevention of Sexual and Domestic Violence was founded in 1977. Its mission is to mobilize the resources of the religious communities to address the widespread problems of sexual and domestic violence. To this end, the Center provides educational and training resources to denominations, local congregations, and individuals who are concerned about preventing abuse and violence.

In response to an urgent need for prevention work with teenagers, the Center produced a curriculum titled *Sexual Abuse Prevention: A Study for Teenagers* in 1984. It was published by United Church Press, New York. Now in its third printing, it has been used throughout the United States in helping teenagers in church youth groups understand and be prepared to deal with sexual abuse.

Subsequently, we began receiving requests for Sunday school curricula for grades four through six. Again, the concern here is that children receive information about sexual abuse in the context of religious instruction. Many public schools now offer prevention material to children. But our concern is that, in addition to the facts about sexual abuse and how to respond to it, our children receive a theological and biblical foundation for their understanding. The very fact that they will hear about sexual abuse in Sunday school or vacation Bible school is a powerful message to them that the church cares about this all-too-common fact of life.

This curriculum, *Preventing Child Sexual Abuse: A Curriculum for Children Ages Nine Through Twelve,* was developed over two years through consultation with an advisory group made up of religious educators from various Christian denominations. Portions of it have been field tested in Sunday schools. It is provided here as a resource to religious educators who intend to expand their ministry with children to include this much-needed information.

The Center for the Prevention of Sexual and Domestic Violence believes that the widespread suffering experienced by victims of sexual and domestic violence represents a profound violation of persons created in God's image. The church's traditional silence has enabled it to live with the illusion that "these things don't happen to good Christian children." But they do. And our denial only means that our children suffer and grow up to be victimized again or to victimize others. These experiences of personal violence and abuse cry out for justice and for a compassionate response from the community of faith. This curriculum is a contribution to our common ministry of justice-making and healing.

Introduction

The Problem

In recent years, our society has begun to understand the pervasiveness of child sexual abuse. It is estimated that one female child out of every three will be sexually abused before she is eighteen years old.[1] In addition, one male child out of every eleven will be sexually abused as well.[2] Child sexual abuse is not confined to any racial, ethnic, or socio-economic class. Children across the world experience the nightmare of abuse.

Only now are we beginning to research the effects of abuse on children. We already know that children who are abused may grow up to abuse others. A survey of San Quentin Federal Prison inmates found that every inmate surveyed had been abused as a child.[3] Some estimate that 75 percent of all adolescents involved in prostitution, both female and male, were victims of prior sexual violence: rape, incestuous abuse, or molestation.[4] Over 50 percent of juvenile sex offenders were sexually or physically abused as children.[5] The abuse experienced by children, especially young children, appears to explode into countless emotional problems that affect everyone in our society.

As our awareness of the effects of child sexual abuse grows, frustrated parents and educators look for ways that we can prevent the abuse from happening to children. In order to teach prevention techniques, we are forced to examine our social, cultural, and religious attitudes about sex roles, family life, sexuality, and violence. The continuing patterns of abuse can be broken with the use of preventive education and with appropriate counseling interventions with children who have already been victimized.

The Response: Religious Education that Teaches Prevention

Education is an important aspect of effectively preventing the sexual abuse of children and adolescents. Education accomplishes the following:

- It breaks through the individual and societal silence and denial that have long supported and tolerated sexual abuse of children and adolescents.
- It increases access to community resources for treatment and intervention by young people.
- It decreases the level of public acceptance of sexual abuse.
- It increases the degree of understanding and awareness by adolescents (or preadolescents) of the issues related to sexual violence.[6]

Prevention education is necessary on two levels: short-term and long-term. The focus of short-term prevention is the dissemination of factual information about rape, incest, and child sexual abuse and the development of skills to enable an individual to avoid or to resist an approach by an offender. Another necessary ingredient for education is information about what to do and whom to contact for help if assaulted. Long-term prevention has to do with institutional and societal change directed at the root causes of sexual abuse. The focus is on an examination of the role that basic cultural attitudes and practices play in supporting and encouraging violence, particularly against the most vulnerable members of society: women, children, youth, and the elderly.[7]

Even though many schools are introducing prevention curricula, it is essential that the church get involved in the prevention of sexual abuse. Our tradition and scripture clearly mandate the necessity of care for those members of our society who are most vulnerable. Jesus' words remind us that as Christians we must publicly stand in solidarity with victims and help in the healing process.

In addition, it is important that the church no longer allow its institutions or scripture to be used to promote violence. Misinterpreted scripture or sermons are frequently used by offenders to justify sexual violence. Therefore, every avenue of communication must be used to spread the gospel message of God's love and care for children.

Purpose of this Course

Young people between the ages of nine and twelve are an important audience for abuse prevention education for several reasons:

- Sexual abuse often begins in early childhood.
- Pre-adolescence is an especially vulnerable time because of the pressure that our society places on children to grow up quickly.
- Pre-adolescents, like adolescents, are very susceptible to the influence of the media and advertising as part of their socializaton as males and females. Here they find a distorted and limited view of relationships, sex roles, and sexuality.
- Children between the ages of nine and twelve may have already been abused sexually either by a family member or by a friend or acquaintance. If so, they need information and permission to seek help in order to break out of their isolation and private pain.

This course has been written to provide information about sexual abuse and its prevention to children between the ages of nine and twelve in the context of a religious education program. Many pre-adolescents either have been victims of sexual abuse or have friends who have experienced abuse.

The purpose of this curriculum is to provide sexual abuse prevention materials to be used specifically in churches as part of a religious education program. The thirteen sessions fit into a typical Sunday morning church school program. However, the material could also be used as curriculum for a special event, perhaps summer Vacation Bible School, after-school programs, or camping programs. The material is written for a limited age group, and therefore it is developmentally geared at age-appropriate levels.

The curriculum draws on excellent secular materials in the field, while at the same time using biblical materials as resources. This material also confronts misinterpretations of biblical materials that have been used to support abusive relationships. Even if a child has had abuse prevention in school, it is important that religious and theological ideas be discussed and examined. Through the church's education program, prevention techniques can be taught in an environment of God's caring and in a supportive community.

Human Sexuality Education

A sexual abuse prevention curriculum should not be confused with human sexuality education. Nor should it take the place of a course that gives information about sexuality. Children ages nine through twelve, depending on their educational system and their parents, may or may not have clear and factual information about their bodies.

Ideally, a religious education sexuality course would be a prerequisite to this material. It would be helpful if each group member had information as well as a sense of positive sexuality. However, this material has been written in such a way that group members can learn abuse prevention techniques without necessarily having a specific course in sexuality. Depending on their background, group members will have questions about both sexual abuse and sexuality. It is important that the leaders answer these questions directly and openly.

Theology and Sexual Abuse Prevention

Many texts in the Bible speak to modern-day readers about God's support and care for victims. Yet victims of abuse themselves often raise challenges as they question our concepts of an all-powerful God, authority, and forgiveness. It is only natural that victims of violence look for answers to these basic religious questions that all humankind struggles to answer: "Why does God allow suffering?" "Why did this happen to me?"

In addition to questions about basic theological concepts, the stories from women and men who have survived abuse often tell us of the comforting power of God. Images of God as comforter and healer helped them survive and helped them heal.

Certainly the words of Luke speak clearly:

Jesus opened the book and found the place where it was written,
"The Spirit of God [or the Lord] is upon me,
because God has anointed me to preach good news to the poor,
and has sent me to proclaim release to the captives
and recovering of sight to those who are blind,
to set at liberty those who are oppressed,
to proclaim the acceptable year of the Sovereign [or Lord]."
And Jesus closed the book, and gave it back to the attendant, and sat down; and the eyes of all in the synagogue were fixed on Jesus, who began to say to them, "Today this scripture has been fulfilled in your hearing."
[Luke 4:16–21a, I-LL]

"To set at liberty those who are oppressed" reminds us of God's power and our responsibility to bring healing to the victim.

Unfortunately, most churches are not prepared to help victims of sexual violence. Our teachings are misinterpreted by offenders. Our sermons too many times leave the victim feeling like God is punishing him or her for past sins and offenses. Even when we want to help, we lack the skills to effectively help victims of violence.

Our religious education programs, established to teach our children our Christian values, reflect our lack of attention to issues of sexual violence. Nothing is more moving than to look at a church filled with small, happy children and remember the overpowering statistics about sexual violence in this country. One out of every three girls and one of every eleven boys will experience the nightmare of sexual violence. How many of the children in our church school classes already have experienced abuse? How many of their friends at school have experienced abuse?

This curriculum is written specifically as a response from the Christian community to the pervasive sexual violence that our children experience. It is not enough that school systems teach sexual abuse prevention, because it is our task in religious education programs to teach our children more than factual information about abuse. Rather, it is our task to teach children that God loves each child, that God is a comforter to those that suffer, that the church is God's community of people who care for others, and that each of us, both male and female, is created in God's image.

That is why it is so important that Bible study, worship, and prayer are included in each and every session. This is not just redone secular material. Rather, our theology stands at the core of this curriculum. This curriculum reflects our basic belief that we are all created in God's image, that children are special to God, and that God seeks justice for the victim and repentance for the offender.

This curriculum is also rooted in the theological concept that all people, both male and female, are created in God's image. It is therefore essential that our theology be inclusive of all people, both male and female. Scriptures cited are basically from the *Inclusive-Language Lectionary,* Revised Standard Version.

Planning for This Course

The curriculum unit is organized into thirteen sessions, a complete quarter-of-year curriculum. It is designed for teaching within a compact series of meetings (such as Vacation Bible School) or in consecutive weekly meetings (such as Sunday morning church school). If time is not available to teach all thirteen sessions, it is recommended that a minimum of the first ten sessions, plus the thirteenth session as closing, be included.

Each session is divided into three sections:

> Getting Started
> Developing the Session
> Concluding the Session

In addition to teaching objectives and a variety of activities, the lessons contain theological concepts, scriptures, prayers, songs, and other forms of worship experiences for young people.

One unique aspect of this material is that the lessons include **ACTIVITY SHEETS** and **FOR YOUR NOTEBOOK** pages, and most may be reproduced. These sheets are to be collected into a student book that each group member can take home at the end of the unit.

The lessons are designed to involve group members, so that they may learn through participation in small group activities, questions, and general discussions. Stories and a film (Session 8) are also included. The film needs to be ordered in advance and previewed.

Session Topics

Session 1: Each Child Is a Child of God
Session 2: God's Gift of Feelings
Session 3: The Rights of Children
Session 4: God Wants You To Be Safe
Session 5: Good Touch/Bad Touch/Confusing Touch
Session 6: God Cares About Us
Session 7: What About the Family?
Session 8: Saying "No!"
Session 9: No More Secrets
Session 10: Justice and Forgiveness: Responding to Harm
Session 11: Peer Pressure
Session 12: Advertising/Males and Females in Media
Session 13: Wrapping it Up With a Positive Self-Image

Leadership

Even when a teacher has a great deal of experience teaching in a church school program, it is highly recommended that the individual have some special training with abuse prevention techniques. Training can be obtained by attending different workshops on child sexual abuse. Another resource is local training groups for public school teachers, like Child Abuse Prevention (CAP), or other similar organizations. If training is not possible, then it is important that the teachers at least be familiar with the topic of sexual abuse. (See **RESOURCES.)**

Given the present scope of child sexual abuse in our society, it is most probable that at least one group member will either have experienced some kind of abuse or will know of someone who has. Therefore, it is essential that each leader knows what to do and how to respond if group members disclose abuse they have suffered. (See Appendix C—How To Help Child Victims.)

Naturally, it is important that the teachers are themselves comfortable with discussing such topics as body parts, sexual violence, incest, assault, and sexual intercourse. It is essential that the group members feel comfortable discussing these issues with the teacher. A teacher who knows the group members well has an advantage.

It is recommended that a team of two people teach the curriculum. It is best if a male-female team of teachers work together. This allows for flexibility in dividing into smaller groups. There may be a big difference in the maturity, sophistication, and experience of children ages nine through twelve. Depending on the maturity of the group, the larger group may need to be divided along gender lines. For different activities, the male or female leaders can take different roles or lead different small groups.

Although sexual abuse takes place in almost all cultures, some cultural factors can influence teaching sexual abuse prevention. For example, in many Asian cultures, the authority of the father is never to be questioned. Therefore, teaching children to say "No!" to an abusive father runs against the values of the culture. Although this curriculum has been written for children in a broad spectrum of cultures, it is impossible to take into account all cultural influences in sexual abuse—authority in the family, forgiveness, justice, and other issues—in this curriculum. It is, therefore, important that the leader recognize the various cultures represented in the group of children. The leader should be prepared to recognize cultural aspects that challenge or enhance teaching of sexual abuse prevention.

More and more educators are becoming aware of the importance of sexual abuse prevention. Any leaders who have new ideas or creative uses of ideas and activities are asked to share their experience by writing to The Center for the Prevention of Sexual and Domestic Violence, 1914 N. 34th St., Suite 105, Seattle, WA 98103.

Preparing the Church for the Child Sexual Abuse Prevention Curriculum

An important task of the adult leaders of this curriculum is to prepare the church for use of these materials in church school classes. Many churches have not had the opportunity to discuss and learn about child sexual abuse. Therefore, the adult leaders need to introduce the topic to both the parents and the entire congregation.

The congregation can be prepared by having announcements in newsletters and bulletins about the future use of these materials. Some churches find that it is a great opportunity to have an adult education class before or even during the use of this material with children. Finally, it can be very helpful if the pastor and other leaders of the church make public and private affirmations that support the use of this material.

Parents' Meeting

Although most parents are very appreciative of having child sexual abuse prevention materials available to their children in a church school setting, some parents have concerns or would like more details about the material. Before the unit of sessions begins, it is important that parents and other adults in the church have an opportunity to look at the materials and learn more about the material. This would also be a great time to preview the film with the parents.

It is strongly recommended that the leaders arrange to meet with parents and other interested adults. This provides an opportunity for parents to be educated first and alerted to some of the material that their children will be learning. Parents will then be better prepared to respond to the questions and concerns that their children voice. Such a meeting also provides an opportunity for parents to raise any questions about the content of the course. Material on sexual abuse may raise some parents' concerns and resistance about sexuality education. A clear explanation of what will be presented usually addresses the concerns and minimizes resistance. Most parents are grateful that their children will be getting this important information. Appendix A contains an information sheet on sexual abuse that can be copied and handed out.

Parents should not attend sessions with children. Some children may be reluctant to discuss sexual abuse in front of their parents. An explanation of this can be made at the parents' meeting and is usually understood by parents. If the parents have enough interest, this might be a great opportunity to have a parents' class on the same topic.

Sample Parent Letter

Dear Parent,

Increasingly, parents are concerned about their children's safety. In particular, sexual abuse is a great concern to parents. The statistics are staggering. One out of every three girls and one out of every eleven boys will be molested before the age of eighteen. Each year, over 100,000 young people are sexually assaulted in our country. [Name of church] is committed to being a community that cares for children. Therefore, we are providing several opportunities for families to learn more about how to prevent sexual assault.

During the next months, [name of church school class] will be studying a special church school curriculum on preventing child sexual abuse. As parents concerned about the safety of your children, we want you to be informed about all aspects of this program. We are providing a Christian educational program that teaches children about God's constant care, trains children to recognize and deal with potentially dangerous situations, and teaches children about resources in our community and within our church to help children who have been hurt.

In addition to the Sunday morning classes for the children, we are offering a workshop on [date] at [time] for parents and other interested adults. This workshop will include information on child sexual abuse, communication tips on talking to your child, and a description of the children's classes.

You are urged to attend this adult workshop. Your questions or concerns could be helpful to us. We hope that you will encourage your child to participate in church school classes during [dates]. If you are unable to attend the adult workshop and you have questions concerning this unit, please feel free to call me.

Sincerely yours,

Session 1

Each Child is a Child of God

Objectives

- To increase participants' knowledge about body integrity.
- To increase participants' understanding that people, both male and female, are created in God's image as bodily beings.
- To help participants begin to understand that some touching is not appropriate.

Theological and Biblical Concepts

In Genesis 1:26–31, God's creation is declared as good. Human beings are part of that creation and also affirmed as being good. All too often, we forget that the goodness of creation includes our bodies as well as our minds and spirits. Our bodies are part of God's creation. This session teaches children that they are unique creations of God and that God loves them. Each of us owns his or her body. Our bodies are to be cared for as part of God's creation.

Resources needed

Decorated box that can be placed in an accessible place for group members in which any written questions can be placed.

    Name tags and markers
    Newsprint or chalkboard
    Copies of Activity Sheets 1-3
    Copies of pages **FOR YOUR NOTEBOOK,** PAGES 24-27
    Crayons and markers for drawing pictures
    Notebook for collecting activity sheets and **FOR YOUR NOTEBOOK** pages

---

This Session in Brief

Getting Started (10 minutes)
    Introduce the Course
    Set Ground Rules

Developing the Session
    Body Integrity (10 minutes)
    Activity: Memory Game

We Are Part of God's Creation and God's Creation is Good (15 Minutes)
My Body Belongs to Me (15 minutes)

Concluding the Session (10 minutes)
Summarize and Evaluate
Invite Questions
Closing

Session Plan

Getting Started

Introduce the Course

- Begin class by introducing yourself to the class. You may know some of the group members and their families through your experience of teaching or other roles that you have in the church.
- Pass out markers and name tags explaining that we need to be able to call each person by her/his name. Ask each person to introduce themselves to the group. If you are new to the group or there are visitors present, ask the members to give the group information about themselves.
- Explain that the topic of this special church school course will be preventing sexual assault and abuse. Ask the group members if they know anything about these topics. Listen carefully to their responses, because many children already have ideas, some accurate and some inaccurate, about what sexual assault is. Ask the group how many of them have had a special class at school about sexual assault. Explain that the church is supposed to be a place for help and healing. Therefore, it is a good place to learn more about protecting yourself and what to do if you need help. Explain that the group will have lots of chances to ask questions about this topic.

Set Ground Rules

- Go over your course plans briefly.
- Explain that asking questions is important.
- Remind the group that listening carefully to each person is important so that everyone understands what is being said.
- Tell the group that the teachers are available between sessions to talk about anything in this course.

NOTE TO THE LEADER

It is very important that trusted adults be available for group members between sessions. Teachers may give the group their home phone numbers. Also, it is important that the teachers be available to talk immediately after the session.

Developing the Session

Body Integrity

Ask the group if it is possible for two people to be exactly alike. Many of the children will say that twins can be alike. Tell them that even twins are not *exactly* alike. Even identical twins are a little different. Some twins like different kinds of music or get different grades in school. Each person is special and unique.

NOTE TO THE LEADER

Many church school classes will be ongoing classes that have been together for most of the school year. However, other classes will be newly formed for this specific course. Classes that have been together for a longer time do not need much time to get acquainted. New classes need more time before plunging into this material. If the group is newly formed, it is suggested that the teacher insert a get-acquainted game before the memory game or a short activity to help group members meet each other. For example: in diads, ask each person to find out three things about a partner and then share it with the group.

Activity: Memory Game

1. Ask the group to number (1, 2, 1, 2) and form a circle.
2. Form an inner circle by asking the 1s to step into the center and face a 2.
3. Give the inner circle thirty seconds to memorize everything about the person facing them. Look carefully at their face, their clothing, jewelry, etc.
4. Ask the group that memorized to turn their backs for a few seconds so that others can change two things about themselves.
5. Have the inner circle turn around and try to guess what the person facing them has changed.
6. Let the outer circle have a turn.

Discussion of Game

Take a few minutes to discuss with the group what they learned from the memory game.

- What changes were easy to notice?
- What changes were hard to notice?
- What characteristics of a person do you notice first?
- What characteristics do all people share?

We Are Part of God's Creation and God's Creation Is Good

Read the creation account in Genesis 2:26–31 (**FOR YOUR NOTEBOOK**). Discuss this passage with the group.

- Notice that humans are an important part of the creation story.
- Point out that males and females are made in the image of God.
- God declares that all of the creation, including humans, is good.

Ask group members to name one thing that they like about their body. Ask the group:

- Do you like your feet?
- What about your hands?
- Name a good thing about your face.

Activity

Give each group a copy of **Activity Sheet 1** on which to draw a picture of their whole self. They should be encouraged to draw themselves any way they choose. Pay attention to the details that they include. Explain that their picture will be included in a book that they can take home at the end of the course.

NOTE TO THE LEADER

Drawing a picture of themselves at this age can take an extended period of time. It might be useful to have the group draw pictures while continuing the discussion. Another idea is to play music while the group draws. This may also help the group relax during this first session.

If a child has such low self-esteem that he or she cannot make an affirming statement about his or her self and draws a very negative image, encourage the child to tell you about the characteristic or aspect of his or her self that he or she likes best.

"My Body Belongs to Me!"

Ask the group members if they can name the parts of a person's body. They will name legs, hands, arms, etc. Some may even name private parts like "bottom," "booty," "wee-wee." Expect them to include some of these parts. Do not show any embarrassment, as they may be testing you. If slang terms are suggested for body parts, ask the group members if they know the correct term for the body part.

Ask if they know what "private parts" are. If they don't know, suggest that private parts are the parts of the body that are covered by a swimsuit or by underwear. Explain that it is *not OK* for an adult or an older child to touch a child's private parts except for health and safety reasons. It is *not OK* for someone a child loves to touch his or her private parts. Explain that it is *not OK* for an adult or an older child to ask a child to touch an adult's or older child's private parts.

Explain to the group that there are times when touching is appropriate. Touching can be necessary for health and safety reasons. Ask the group to give examples of when it is OK to touch private parts:

- doctors with a nurse or parent present;
- parents in special situations;
- when you wash yourself.

Explain that our bodies are our gift to explore:

- It is OK to touch yourself;
- It is important to take care of yourself;
- You are responsible for self-care.

Explain that it is NEVER OK for a grown-up to touch a child's private parts if the grown-up makes it a secret. Tell the group that their body belongs to them. Hand out **Activity Sheet 2** to add to the student books.

NOTE TO THE LEADER

During the various activities in these sessions, the adult leader may find it advantageous to divide the group by gender. If the group is immature, group members may be more comfortable being in a small group composed of group members of the same gender. It may be better for the girls to be separated from the boys. Some activities are recommended for groups divided by gender. Most activities, however, are recommended for the entire group, or for mixed-gender small groups.

More Bible

Read passages from Psalm 8 **(FOR YOUR NOTEBOOK)** about the goodness of the creation of humans. Discuss this passage:

- Notice that humans are called "little less than God."
- Point out how the passage says that humans are so important to God that God remembers and cares for them.

Read 1 Corinthians 3:16 **(FOR YOUR NOTEBOOK)** about the body being the temple of God. Discuss this passage:

- Notice that a person's body is God's temple.
- A temple is a place where God's spirit dwells.
- What are some ways to take care of the temple?

Concluding the Session

Summarize and Evaluate

Gather the group together for a time to share discoveries made in this session. Describe plans for the next session.

Invite Questions

Show the group the question box set in a place where everyone has access to it. Explain that this box is for them to put any questions in that they would like to have the teacher answer. Tell the group that their parents received a letter about this class. Suggest that they might want to find a trusted adult, perhaps a parent or someone else, to talk to further about the topics that are discussed in this course.

Closing

Introduce the song printed on **Activity Sheet 3.** This song can be a theme song for the entire course. Use this song in the introduction or closing of any session.
Discuss the meaning of the words of the song with the group.

NOTE TO THE LEADER

The chances are very good that your group will have one or more children who have been sexually abused or are being sexually abused. This course is written to help children protect themselves, and it is possible that a child might disclose their own or a friend's abuse. Every session should include an invitation to disclose this abuse privately. The children should be reminded that the teacher is available and that there are also trusted adults who will want to talk to them.

For Your Notebook

Then God said, "Let us make humans in our image, after our likeness; and let them have dominion over the fish of the sea, and over the birds of the air, and over the cattle, and over all the earth, and over every creeping thing that creeps upon the earth." So God created humans in God's own image, in the image of God God created; male and female God created them. And God blessed them, and God said to them, "Be fruitful and multiply, and fill the earth and subdue it; and have dominion over the fish of the sea and over the birds of the air and over every living thing that moves upon the earth." And God said, "Behold, I have given you every plant yielding seed which is upon the face of all the earth, and every tree with seed in its fruit; you shall have them for food. And to every beast of the earth, and to every bird of the air, and to everything that creeps on the earth, everything that has the breath of life, I have given every green plant for food." And it was so. And God saw everything that God had made, and behold, it was very good. And there was evening and there was morning, a sixth day.

[RSV]

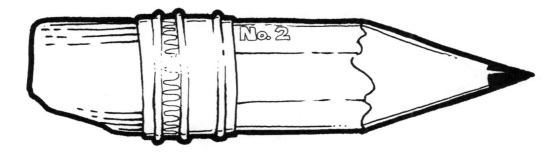

I AM SPECIAL TO GOD. THIS IS A PICTURE OF ME!

ACTIVITY SHEET 2

It is not OK for a grown-up or an older child to touch your private parts. Even if the grown-up is someone you love, the grown-up should not touch your private parts except for health and safety reasons. For example, it is OK for a doctor to give you a check-up to be sure that you are well.

- It is never OK for a grown-up or an older child to touch a child's private parts and make it a secret.
- It is not OK for a grown-up or an older child to ask a child to touch the grown-up's or other child's private parts.

(Permission is given to reproduce this page for students.)

For Your Notebook
[optional]

Psalm 8

O Sᴏᴠᴇʀᴇɪɢɴ, our God,
   how majestic is your name in all the earth!
You whose glory above the heavens is chanted
   by the mouths of babes and infants,
you have founded a bulwark because of your foes,
   to still the enemy and the avenger.
When I look at your heavens, the work of your fingers,
   the moon and the stars which you have established;
what are human beings that you are mindful of them,
   and mortals that you care for them?
Yet you have made them little less than God,
   and crowned them with glory and honor.
You have given them dominion over the works of your hands,
   you have put all things under their feet,
all sheep and oxen,
   and also the beasts of the field,
the birds of the air, and the fish of the sea,
   whatever passes along the paths of the sea.
O Sᴏᴠᴇʀᴇɪɢɴ, our God,
   how majestic is your name in all the earth!   [I-LL]

1 Corinthians 3:16–17

Do you not know that you are God's temple and that God's spirit dwells in you? Whoever destroys God's temple, God will destroy. For God's temple is holy, and you are that temple.   [I-LL]

ACTIVITY SHEET 3

"I Am a Promise"

W. J. G. and Gloria Gaither

William J. Gaither

Session 2

God's Gift of Feelings

Objectives

- To increase participants' awareness that feelings are a resource for response to the world.
- To be able to name and describe one's feelings.
- To increase participants' understanding that feelings are part of God's creation and clues about what has happened to us.

Theological and Biblical Concepts

Throughout the gospels, Jesus expressed a range of emotions. He experienced anger, sadness, and happiness. Jesus felt all kinds of feelings, just as we do.

As with Jesus, we too feel a range of emotions. In some situations, we feel happy and joyful. In other situations, we feel anger and rage. It is important that children understand that feelings are also part of God's creation. Feelings are good, and they are clues to help us understand our situation. Feelings are sometimes clues that warn us that we are in danger.

Resources Needed

Bibles
Markers and crayons
Newsprint/poster board
Copies of Activity Sheets 4 and 5

This Session in Brief

Getting Started (10 minutes)
Build Community
Questions and Answers

Developing the Session
Jesus and Feelings (20 minutes)
Trust Your Feelings (20 minutes)

Concluding the Session (10 minutes)
Summarize and Evaluate
Closing

Session Plan

Getting Started

Build Community

- Ask each member of the group to share the picture that they drew of themselves last session. If they don't feel comfortable sharing, ask the group members why it might be uncomfortable to share in this group. Share that sometimes this is true for many people.

Questions and Answers

- Check the question box to see if there are any questions that the group members have left for the teacher. You may not know the answers to the questions, but assure the group that you will do your best to get answers. If there are any questions that you can answer, do your best to give accurate information. Ask the group if they have any questions that they can think of now that they want to ask.

Developing the Session

Jesus and Feelings

Copy the following scriptures on newsprint or poster board.

John 11:32-35

Then Mary, when she came and saw Jesus, fell at his feet, and said, "Sovereign [or Lord], if you had been here, my brother would not have died." When Jesus saw her weeping, and the Jews who came with her also weeping, he was indignant in spirit and troubled, and said, "Where have you laid Lazarus?" They answered, "Sovereign [or Lord], come and see." Jesus wept [I-LL].

Matthew 21:12-13

And Jesus entered the temple of God and drove out all who sold and bought in the temple, and he overturned the tables of the money-changers and the seats of those who sold pigeons. He said to them, "It is written, 'My house shall be called a house of prayer; but you make it a den of robbers'" [RSV].

Ask group members to look up the scriptures. Discuss each scripture:

- How does Jesus feel in each situation?
- Have you ever felt as Jesus felt?

Trust Your Feelings

Tell the group that God has given each person feelings. For example, when a pet is sick, we feel bad. But at a birthday party, most of us feel happy. What are some of the different kinds of feelings that people have? The group should name feelings like: scared, surprised, excited, confused, etc.

Activity: Activity Sheet 4

NOTE TO THE LEADER

Group members may feel very differently in the same situation. Always remember that all feelings should be validated. There are no correct answers. For example, some members may find the darkness comforting and quiet, whereas others find it scary and frightening.

Remind the group of the previous session about body integrity. Emphasize the guidelines again. (It might be helpful to print these guidelines on a newsprint and hang them on the wall.)

- It is not OK for an adult or older child to touch a child's private parts except for health and safety reasons.
- It is not OK for an adult or older child to ask a child to touch the adult's or older child's private parts.

Explain that feelings sometimes help us know what to do. Examples include:

- When a car comes really fast down the road, we probably would feel a little scared and move away from the road.
- Or if we found a kitten trapped in a tree, we would probably feel sorry for the kitten and get help.

Ask the group for other examples of situations when they might experience feelings that would tell them what to do.

Tell the group that sometimes it is hard to know whether touching is OK or not. Feelings are clues that give us hints about what to do. Ask the group what are some clues that it is OK for an adult to touch a younger person's private parts. Some answers might be:

- The adult cares about the younger person.
- The younger person feels respected.
- The younger person feels like he or she can say "no!" and he or she won't be forced.
- The younger person feels like a trusted adult can be there.
- The adult has a medical reason.
- The younger person feels safe.

Activity: Activity Sheet 5
Ask the group to share some of their answers.

Concluding the Session

Summarize and Evaluate
Provide time for the group to talk about what they have discovered in this session.

NOTE TO THE LEADER

Several closing experiences involve beginning steps for the group to learn relaxation techniques. These techniques are the beginning steps for learning meditation. The group needs to be encouraged to gradually relax and enjoy the silence. The silence is most conducive to listening to our inner voice and sorting out our feelings.

Closing

Trusting our feelings involves listening to our inner voice and listening to God. Prayer is one way that we communicate with God and also think through our own feelings. Close this group session by asking the group to have a period of relaxation and silence. Finish with a prayer.

Ask each group member to find a place to lie down (It would be a good idea to provide towels or sheets of paper for each member of the group.) If the group has no experience with meditation, it might be best to ask the group to sit quietly rather than lying down. Explain that the group will have a few minutes of silence. Remind the group to breathe deeply. Deep breathing is important if group members are to feel comfortable. During this time we will be thinking about how we are feeling.

Explain that the questions asked are not to be answered out loud; rather they serve to give each person something to think about.

- Are you breathing deeply? How does that breathing make you feel?
- Do you have your eyes open or closed?
- When you close your eyes, does it make you feel more alone?
- Can you feel your heart beating?
- Is your heart beating fast, slowly, or in between?
- Think of a time when you felt really proud.
- Where were you?
- Who was with you?

Prayer: O God, you have given us many feelings. Sometimes we are scared, and we ask you to be with us. Sometimes we feel sad, and we know that you care about how we are feeling. Sometimes we feel happy, and we want to celebrate with you. Help us to use our feelings to tell us what your will is in our lives. Amen.

33

For Your Notebook

Activity Sheet 4
Sentence Finishers

When my parent tickles me, I feel. . .

When I hold a puppy, I feel. . .

If I stole money, I would feel. . .

When I am in a haunted house at Halloween, I feel. . .

When I eat cold ice cream, I feel. . .

When I play on a beach in the summer, I feel. . .

When I get all my homework done, I feel. . .

When my team wins a soccer game, I feel. . .

When I ask someone to stop and he or she won't, I feel. . .

When someone cheats in a game, I feel. .

When I am in the dark, I feel. . .

When a friend jumps out from behind the door, I feel. . .

When someone gives me a present, I feel. . .

When I talk on the phone to a friend, I feel. . .

When friends won't stop teasing me, I feel. . .

Activity Sheet 5

What are clues that it's not OK for an adult or an older child to touch you?

• when the adult says that the touching is a secret
• when the adult frightens the younger person
• when the younger person feels uncomfortable
• when the adult won't stop when you say "no."

Fill in the blank lines:

• when_____

• when_____

• when_____

• when_____

(Permission is given to reproduce this page for students.)

Session 3

The Rights of Children

Objectives

- To increase participants' awareness that as children they have rights that include the right to say "No" to an adult.
- To increase participants' awareness that for every right there is a corresponding responsibility.
- To increase participants' awareness that Jesus valued children.

Theological and Biblical Concepts

Throughout his ministry, Jesus emphasized how special children are. Matthew 19:13-15 tells us about the children being brought to Jesus. The disciples were going to send them away, but Jesus said, "Let the children come to me, and do not hinder them; for to such belongs the kingdom of heaven."

In a very straightforward manner, Jesus shows us the special place that those who are younger and smaller have in our community. Rather than telling the children to be like adults, Jesus tells the adults that they should become like the children, because children have a special place in the reign of God.

Because of this specialness, children have rights. The creation story in Genesis 1:26-31 (Session 1) also reminds us that each person has a responsibility to self and others. All of creation is good, and humans have the responsibility to take care of ourselves and creation. Children grow into this responsibility.

Resources Needed

Chalkboard and chalk or newsprint and markers
Bibles
Slips of paper and pencils
Copies of **FOR YOUR NOTEBOOK**, pages 39–41

This Session in Brief

Getting Started (10 minutes)
Build Community
Questions and Answers

Developing the Session
Everyone Has Rights (20 minutes)
Rights and Responsibilities (20 minutes)

Concluding the Session (10 minutes)
Summarize and Evaluate
Closing

Session Plan

Getting Started

Building Community
Begin this session by asking the group about the one main thing that they remember from the last session.

Questions and Answers
Check the question box to see if there are any questions.

Developing the Session

Jesus and Children

- Explain that during Jesus' time, children were thought of as property. Children had no rights. Even until the last century, children had no rights in this country. Often, children had to work long hours in factories and in the fields, because they supported their families.
- Jesus taught that children are special and need special care.
- Read Matthew 19:13-15 **(FOR YOUR NOTEBOOK)**.

Rights
Lead a discussion about the rights of people.

- What are rights?
- Are the rights of adults different from the rights of children?
- Do men and women have the same rights?
- Do people in other countries have rights too?
- Do rights come from the government or from God?
- List the rights of children. (Use a chalkboard or newsprint and markers.)
- Compare the group's list of rights with the list **For Your Notebook,** page 40.

Responsibilities
Lead a discussion about the responsibilities of younger persons.

- What are responsibilities?
- Are the responsibilities of an adult different from the responsibilities of children?
- List the responsibilities that correspond to the rights that were listed in the first part of this lesson. (Use chalkboard or newsprint paper.)
- Compare the group's list of responsibilities with the list in **For Your Notebook,** page 41.

In addition to these responsibilities, each person has a responsibility to respect the rights of others. Therefore, remind the group members that they should never force another person to be touched or to touch their private parts.

NOTE TO THE LEADER

Throughout these sessions, it is important to remember that children, even at this young age, have sometimes already been or have the potential to become abusers themselves. Sometimes the experience of being abused or other trauma affects children in such a way that they use power over a younger child to build up their own self-esteem. The class bully is an example of a child who intimidates and uses power over others. Some children, at a very young age, begin sexually molesting other smaller or younger children. It is therefore important that the teacher not only discuss saying "No!" to a potentially abusive situation, but that the teacher also discuss the responsibility of all human beings to take care of those who are smaller and younger. However, sexual abuse is not to be confused with "playing doctor". Sexual abuse involves an adult or one child who is older (five or more years) or more powerful forcing or tricking someone younger, smaller, or less powerful to participate in sexual activity.

Emphasize that rights are God's gift to every person. They are something to which every human being is entitled.

Optional Activities
Read *Mine and Yours* by Joy Wilt (Waco, TX: Educational Products, n.d.)

Concluding the Session

Summarize and Evaluate
Ask each member of the group to write a question for the question box. Ask the group for comments and questions that they might have concerning the topic or this course. Describe the plans for the next session.

Closing
Write a group poem. Ask the group for three summary words. Have each group member write one line about each of the three words on a 3″ × 5″ card. (Group members do not need to sign their names.) For example, the words could be "right," "responsibility," and "self." Then each group member would write a sentence about each word, such as: "I have the right to make mistakes."

On newsprint, write the three words. After collecting the cards, write all the sentences to make a poem. Read the finished poem to the group.

NOTE TO THE LEADER

This poem makes a great addition to the booklet that each group member is making. Type out the poem and duplicate it for the next session and for the group members' notebooks. For an additional activity, ask group members to illustrate the group poem.

For Your Notebook

Matthew 19:13-15

Then children were brought to him [Jesus] that he might lay his hands on them and pray. The disciples rebuked the people; but Jesus said, "Let the children come to me, and do not hinder them; for to such belongs the kingdom of heaven." And he laid his hands on them and went away [RSV].

Rights

You have the right to:
  be your own person,
  be honest,
  get your needs met,
  ask questions and obtain honest answers,
  think your own thoughts and believe your own beliefs,
  make mistakes,
  make the decisions and choices that you can and be in on the decisions that
  will affect you,
  own your own things,
  have privacy,
  live free from fear, and
  grow and develop at your own pace.[1]

(Permission is given to reproduce this page for students.)

Responsibilities

If you want to be your own person,
> you have the *responsibility* to allow other people to be their own persons.

If you want to be honest,
> you have the *responsibility* to allow other people to be honest.

If you want to get your needs met,
> you have the *responsibility* of allowing other people to get their needs met.

If you want to ask questions and get honest answers,
> you have the *responsibility* of allowing other people to ask questions and get honest answers.

If you want to think your own thoughts and believe your own beliefs,
> you have the *responsibility* of allowing other people to think their own thoughts and believe their own beliefs.

If you want to make mistakes,
> you have the *responsibility* of allowing other people to make mistakes.

If you want to make choices and decisions and be in on the decisions that affect you,
> you have the *responsibility* of allowing other people to make choices and decisions and be in on the decisions that affect them.

If you want to own your own things,
> you have the *responsibility* of allowing other people to own their own things.

If you want to have privacy,
> you have the *responsibility* of allowing other people to have privacy.

If you want to live a life free from fear,
> you have the *responsibility* of allowing other people to live lives free from fear.

If you want to grow and develop at your own pace,
> you have the *responsibility* of allowing other people to grow and develop at their own paces.[2]

(Permission is given to reproduce this page for students.)

Session 4

God Wants You To Be Safe

Objectives

- To help participants understand child sexual abuse.
- To expand participants' image of God to include the image of God as a source of comfort.

Theological and Biblical Concepts

As a source of comfort, God's activity has been compared to that of a mother hen. In Matthew 23:37, Jesus laments over Jerusalem turning away from God. Jesus uses the metaphor of God being a mother hen who gathers her brood under her wing.

In this scripture, the image of God as a mother hen presents God as a source of comfort. For victims of violence, this image of God can be a source of healing and comfort. God is present with the victims of abuse. It is God's will that people be safe and cared for. Not only is child abuse against the law, it is also against God's will.

Resources Needed

Newsprint or chalkboard
Markers or chalk
Copies of Activity Sheet

This Session in Brief

Getting Started (10 minutes)
Building Community
Questions and Answers

Developing the Session
What is Child Abuse? (10 minutes)
God as a Mother Hen (10 minutes)
Learn Ways to Protect Yourself (10 minutes)
Activity: "What-If" Game (10 minutes)

Concluding the Session (10 minutes)
Summarize and Evaluate
Closing

Emphasize that child abuse is against the law. It is against the law because it hurts children. It is also against God's will. God wants children to be safe.

Background for the Leader

Most adults and children tend to think of child abuse as being only physical endangerment; however, it is important that child abuse be understood to include much more than only physical implications.

Child abuse includes:

- physical abuse and corporal punishment resulting in a traumatic condition,
- emotional abuse,
- physical neglect and/or inadequate supervision, and
- sexual abuse and exploitation.

Call the local Child Abuse Council, or other local resources, about the laws concerning the definition of child abuse in your area.

Session Plan

Getting Started

Building Community
Ask each group member to share his or her nickname and describe the origin of that name.

Questions and Answers
Take each individual question, no matter how silly or serious, and answer as well as you can. (Before coming to class, take a look at the questions so that you have answers ready.)

Developing the Session

What Is Child Abuse?
The adult leader should lead a discussion with the group about child abuse.

- What is child abuse?
- Have any group members ever seen anything about child abuse on television?
- Has anyone ever known anyone who experienced child abuse?

NOTE TO THE LEADER

The adult leader should encourage the group to define abuse themselves. The definition is provided so that the leader can be sure that the definition is correct. It is important that the group members feel they have generated this definition themselves.

It is also important that participants be allowed to share stories they have heard. Children ages nine through twelve have detailed stories concerning experiences of friends, plots from movies, and other sources. Their story-telling gives them a chance to share as well as learn the definitions of abuse.

Sexual Abuse—A Special Kind of Child Abuse

The adult leader should lead a discussion about sexual abuse. Ask the group to define sexual abuse. Write the group's definition and the examples on newsprint or on a chalkboard.

- What is sexual abuse? (A formal definition might include: sexual contact by an adult or older child with a younger child, which can be touching or non-touching.)
- List examples of sexual abuse. Some examples might include when an adult or an older child:
  —touches a child's private parts
  —takes pictures of children's private parts
  —asks a child to touch an adult's or older child's private parts
  —engages in sexual activity, such as kissing on the mouth or having sexual intercourse, with a child.

BACKGROUND FOR THE LEADER

It is important for people to understand why it is wrong for children to be exploited by adults. Sexual contact between an adult and a child is wrong because the child is not developmentally capable of understanding the sexual activity. In addition, the child may not be able to resist the contact. Finally, the child may be psychologically and socially dependent on the offender. Because of these factors, sexual contact between an adult and a child, or sexual contact between an older child and a younger child, is sexual exploitation.

Each teacher should review "Reporting Child Sexual Abuse" in the Appendix D.

God as a Mother Hen
Read Matthew 23:37

O Jerusalem, Jerusalem, killing the prophets and stoning those who are sent to you! How often would I have gathered your children together as a hen gathers her brood under her wings, and you would not! [RSV]

Discuss the scripture.

- How is God described in this scripture?
- Why would a mother hen put the chicks under her wing?
- How does God feel about those who are harmed?
- Can you think of a time when you felt that God was a source of comfort?

Learn Ways to Protect Yourself

- Ask group members what warnings they have learned from their parents and teachers to use in order to protect themselves from people who might hurt them.
- List all the ways they can think of on a chalkboard or on newsprint. Examples might include:
  —Don't get in a car with a stranger.

—Don't walk or play alone in parks.
- Discuss how effective group members think these precautions are.
  —Do these rules work well in a situation where the grown-up is a stranger?
  —How effective are these rules if the grown-up who hurts children is someone the child knows?
- Tell the group that most child abuse takes place between a child and a grown-up that the child knows. This course will help the group members learn ways to protect themselves from grown-ups who hurt children, even when the grown-up is someone they know.
- What are some clues that a person might be in danger?
  —Someone wants a "special" relationship to be a secret.
  —A child feels uncomfortable.
  —Our feelings tell us that something is wrong.

Activity: "What-if" Game[1]

Procedure:

1. Brainstorm about possible responses that individual group members could use when confronted by potentially dangerous situations. Write responses on newsprint or on a chalkboard.

2. Set up two chairs at the front of the room. Tell the class that whoever sits in the one chair will pretend that they are an offender. Whoever sits in the second chair will pretend to be the person that the offender is trying to trick or trap into sexual contact. An adult leader should play the role of the potential offender.

3. The two people in the chairs are to make up a story. The rest of the class will act as referees. The story is made of "What if . . ." statements made by the offender. After two responses from a group member, discuss the choices with the group. Ask another group member to play the part of the child. (An alternative way to play this game is for the teacher to be the offender and for the teacher to solicit responses from the whole group.)

  Example: Offender: What if I followed you home from school?"
  Child: "I'd run as fast as I can."
  Offender: "What if I ran faster than you?"
  Child: "I'd scream and yell like crazy."
  Offender: "What if nobody heard you?"

4. Help the class keep in mind the purpose of this role-play is not to "win." The object is to explore realistic alternatives to possible situations. This probably prohibits the use of machine guns, karate, and other unrealistic tactics.

5. The rest of the class can help you by acting as referees. They may interrupt at points where they feel that either the victim or the offender are being unrealistic, or if either gets stuck. If someone gets stuck, the class may discuss the choices that led to getting stuck.

6. Emphasize that if a child can't find a way out, it is still not his or her fault. It may be that the wisest response to an extremely dangerous situation may be to do nothing until the child is safe and can tell someone.

NOTE TO THE LEADER

Most of the media attention in the last few years has focused on prevention of kidnapping and sexual abuse by strangers. This could be characterized as "stranger danger." However, the statistics show that most children are abused by someone they already know. According to the California Commission on the Status of Women, 80 percent of all cases of child abuse involve the assault of a child by someone he or she knows—a relative, stepparent, family friend, parent, or trusted individual.

Therefore, it is important that discussions of how to prevent sexual abuse always emphasize the difficulty of saying "No!" to a trusted individual, someone the child cares about. It is much easier for discussions to focus on stranger danger, but prevention can only take place when we face the possibility of abuse within our families and among our acquaintances.

Concluding the Session

Summarize and Evaluate
Ask the group to share some ideas learned and feelings about what happened in the session.
Tell the group about future sessions.

Closing

- Ask the group to either stand or sit in a circle and to pray together the reflective prayer on Activity Sheet 6.
- Give each group member a copy of the song from Activity Sheet 6.
- Discuss briefly how this song relates to the story of Jesus and the children and to the topic of this session.

ACTIVITY SHEET 6

Prayer

Comforting God, who is always with us, even when we suffer. We thank you for the good things in our lives. We thank you for trusted adults who care about us. We thank you for good friends.

We pray for children all over the world who are hurt in all the ways that we have learned about today. Be with them. Help us to be a friend to those who are hurt. Amen.

"Jesus Said to All the People"

Ann Evans

GOD LOVES ME 8.7.7.7.7.7.
Swedish Folk Tune

Moderately (♩=96) *in unison*

1. Je-sus said to all the peo-ple As they crowd-ed close to hear,
2. Je-sus said to all the peo-ple As he taught them how to pray,

"God_ loves you as I love you; God is with you ev-'ry-where."
"God_ loves you as I love you; God_ knows the prayers you pray."

Je-sus showed that God_ loves me, God is with me ev-'ry-where.
Je-sus taught that God_ loves me, God_ knows the prayers I pray.

From *Sing to God* (New York: United Church Press, 1984), hymn 23.
"God Loves Me" by Ann Evans, Music arrangement copyright © 1972 by Graded Press. Used by permission.

Session 5

Good Touch/Bad Touch/ Confusing Touch

Objectives

- To increase participants' knowledge about good, bad, and confusing touch.
- To help participants recognize that God intends for us to have touch that is nurturing and affirming.

Theological and Biblical Concepts

In John 10:10 Jesus tells his followers that he is the good shepherd. Unlike a thief that comes to destroy and steal, Jesus reminds us that he came to give life. The Revised Standard Version uses the word "abundantly." Jesus comes to give people life full of goodness.

Session 5 explains the concept of good, bad, and confusing touch. The John 10:10 tells us that Jesus wants us to have an abundant life. Good touch is life-giving and affirming. It is healthy and part of the abundant life that Jesus promises us.

It is important for us to remember that good touch is not just a luxury in life; rather, good touch is essential in life. New babies must have holding and touching in order to survive. Children do not thrive without the touch of others. Throughout the gospels, Jesus touched people. He put his hands on people in a way that healed and comforted. Jesus' touch was life-giving. In this session, the healing, comforting, and affirming aspects of good touch should be emphasized.

Resources Needed

Newsprint and markers, chalkboard and chalk
Magazines
Glue
Scissors
Large piece of cardboard (approximately 36″ by 11″)
3″ × 5″ cards
Copies of Activity Sheets 7 and 8
Copies of **FOR YOUR NOTEBOOK,** page 56

This Session in Brief

Getting Started (5 minutes)
Build Community
Questions and Answers

Developing the Session
Touch Continuum (15 minutes)
Bible Study (15 minutes)
The Right and Wrong of Touching (15 minutes)

Concluding the Session (10 minutes)
Summarize and Evaluate
Closing

Background for the Leader

From Marie Fortune, *Sexual Abuse Prevention: A Study for Teenagers* (New York: United Church Press, 1984) pp. 20-21.

The Touch Continuum (used throughout this session) is designed as an educational tool to assist in explaining the difference between good and bad touch. The Touch Continuum explores such questions as: What is the difference between good and bad touch? When does good or nurturing touch become confusing? When does confusing touch become bad or exploitative?

Touch and how it changes is a grey, confusing area for many adults. As children, few adults had anyone explain different types of touch to them. Instead, many received negative, double, confusing, or non-messages about touch. Negative messages included "Good girls do not touch that way" or "A big boy doesn't touch that way!" Unfortunately, a common double message comes in the form of a parent spanking a child to teach the child not to hit a sibling. Messages become confusing when people do not understand the touch they are given or are asked to give. The touch non-messages are less easy to identify. These are the non-verbal messages received about touch from social and environmental influences.

Based on the responses of elementary students, parents, teens, and professionals, the continuum is designed with four basic components.

Lack of Touch	Nurturing Touch	Confusing Touch	Exploitative Touch	Lack of Touch
1 2	3 4	5 6	7 8	9 10

Lack of touch[1] refers to deprivation of a physical touching stimulation. Lack of touch is included on the continuum because of the various impacts this deprivation can have on people and their sense of touch. Children who were deprived of touch reported feeling unloved or as if something was wrong with them. However, if children are uncomfortable with touching, they shouldn't be forced to do so. Children seemed to find it easier to express physical touch when positive touch role models were available.

Nurturing touch refers to positive expressions of warmth, caring, giving, and physical communication. Most often the receiver of this touch feels as if someone has given to them or has shared with them rather than taken from them.

Positive touch represents itself in many forms. Children were asked to fill in their own examples of "good" touch. To start the students thinking, they were given personal examples or were offered examples such as petting animals, playing games (tag, leapfrog, statue games), kissing, holding hands, cuddling, etc. They were then asked if anything was wrong with this touch and with whom they do this type of touch.

Confusing touch encompasses much of the touch in our society. Touch can be classified as confusing when:

1. The receiver does not understand or misinterprets the intent of the giver.

2. Double messages are perceived between the verbal and physical communication.

3. The touch is not of the nature receiver is used to or familiar with.

4. The touch does not fit or is in conflict with the attitudes, values, or morals of the giver and/or the receiver.

Confusing touch was explained to children in terms of "touch that mixes you up or makes you feel funny, even though there may be nothing wrong with this touch." Another common example was having to kiss someone they did not want to kiss, but they had to to please their parents. Ironically, although the children knew there was nothing wrong with the person who gave them the touch, they also received the non-message that they did not have a right to talk about the kinds of touch they did not like. If children can't discuss their dislike for kissing Uncle Bill because he smells like a cigar and slobbers, how can they speak of more exploitative types of touch?

Exploitative touch refers to manipulation or forced touch. One of the most extreme examples of exploitative touch is rape. Although many forms of exploitative touch are against the law, the laws are not inclusive of all exploitative touch. One example of this is sexual contact between a client and a therapist or any other professional in a position of authority with a client. Another is commonly called "acquaintance rape." Acquaintance rapes (sexual assault of a partner or friend) are not adequately dealt within the legal system. Victims' feelings of self-blame, confusion, and denial complicate existent legal problems.[2]

Session Plan

Getting Started

Build Community
Review the following key words from Session 4: child abuse, physical abuse, emotional abuse, sexual abuse, offender, victim. Describe this session to the group.

Questions and Answers
Answer any questions and check the question box.

NOTE TO THE LEADER

As a leader, you will often get inappropriate responses from the group. Most of these responses are given because the group is uncomfortable or embarrassed

52

by the topic. Sometimes a group member might respond with a silly or "off-the-wall" answer because the topic is difficult to discuss (perhaps because they know someone who is being abused or they themselves are being abused). Don't let the inappropriate responses get you off track, but try to keep working on the topic. If the responses really get out of hand, then discuss with the group why a person might want to give a silly answer, and suggest possible ways for the group to help people give real answers.

Developing the Session

Touch Continuum[3]

1. Define the following terms:

- *Good Touch:* warm and caring touch; makes a person feel affirmed, nurtured, and good about themselves.
- *Bad Touch:* hurtful, manipulative, or forced touch; makes a person feel bad about themselves.
- *Confusing Touch:* makes a person feel uncomfortable, uneasy, confused, unsure about the intentions of the one touching them.

Explain briefly the concept of "continuum," used here to refer to gradations between extremes. For example, hot, cold, warm, cool, and in between. Then describe the Touch Continuum. (See Background for the Leader.)

2. Draw the touch continuum on newsprint or on the chalkboard. Ask group members to recall childhood experiences of touching. (For visual reinforcement, use different colored markers. Use the color red for bad touch, green for good, and brown for confusing.) Place these on the continuum. For example:

NOTE TO THE LEADER

Using the Touch Continuum helps participants to identify and categorize their own experience as well as to affirm their feelings about those experiences. It gives them permission to feel good, bad, or confused about being touched.

Complete Sentence Fragments

Distribute blank 3″ × 5″ index cards to group members. Ask them to complete the following sentences based on their current experience. Write one sentence fragment at a time on the board. After participants have had time to respond, write the next one. Tell them that the cards will be handed in for use, but their responses will be anonymous.

I feel bad when (someone touches me in a certain way).

I feel good when (someone touches me in a certain way).

I feel confused when (someone touches me in a certain way).

Ask them to identify the "someone" by role, not by name, and describe the touch. For example:

"I feel bad when my mother slaps me."

"I feel good when a friend gives me a hug."

"I feel confused when someone I don't know very well puts his arm around me."

Collect the cards. Sorting through quickly, read aloud the most representative examples of each type of touch. Be sure to use any examples of confusing and bad touch in the family or with girlfriends/boyfriends. Write some examples on the continuum on the newsprint.

NOTE TO THE LEADER

Using the response cards and reading the responses aloud helps to break down the individual's sense of isolation. They hear their own experiences in others' responses and yet remain anonymous.

Bible Study
Read John 10:1–10 **(FOR YOUR NOTEBOOK).**
Discuss the text. (See the Theological and Biblical Concepts Section).

- What are some of the characteristics of a shepherd?
- Why would Jesus call himself a shepherd?
- What might "life abundant" mean?
- Can you think of why touching is so important to babies?

The Right and Wrong of Touching[4]
Use the following questions to stimulate group discussion based on the Touch Continuum exercises.

What is wrong about "bad" touch? "Bad" touch makes a person feel bad about themselves. They may feel frightened, powerless, put-down, and exploited because someone they see as more powerful than they are touching them in a particular way or forcing them to do something they don't want to do. It is wrong to touch someone this way, because it takes away that person's right to decide what they want and it makes them feel bad about themselves. It's not wrong because it is sexual; it's wrong because it takes advantage of the other person.

What is right about "good" touch? "Good" touch makes a person feel good about themselves. When someone touches them in a positive and non-exploitive way, they feel affirmed, accepted, respected, supported, and loved. It is touch that both people freely choose. It is right to touch someone in this way, because it affirms the worth of that person as one created in God's image and therefore worthy of acceptance.

Is "good" touch always the right thing to do? It is important to understand that a "good" touch is different from touches that just feel good. People may choose to be touched or to touch another in different ways at different stages in their lives. Circumstances will mean that some touch is appropriate while other touch is not. What may be "good" touch in one relationship wouldn't be in another (a hug from a friend may be "good," but that same hug may be "bad" or uncomfortable from a stranger.) What may be "good" touch at one point in a relationship may be "confusing" or "bad" touch at a later point (for example, a kiss on a cheek from a relative may be "bad" or "confusing" when a person becomes a pre-teen.) "Good" touch (by definition) is never wrong. However, it may not always be the wisest or most appropriate action.

So is "confusing" touch right or wrong? It is mostly confusing because it is never really clear what is going on or why someone is touching you in this way. If the person being touched feels in any way uncomfortable, frightened, or hesitant and really doesn't want to be made to feel these things, then it is wrong to touch them this way.

Sometimes the confusion occurs because a family member is touching another family member. Sometimes touches that felt "good" when a person was a small child feel uncomfortable or frightening as a person grows older. Puberty is a time of change not only of bodies but of feelings, friendships, and relationships at home. It is wrong for an adult to take advantage of a child by touching the child in a way that makes the child feel uncomfortable.

Every person has the right to not be touched in "bad" or "confusing" ways. What are some of the responsibilities of touching? In order to respect the rights of others, it is important never to force someone else to be touched in a way that is "confusing" or "bad." Remember from Session 3 that every right has a matching responsibility.

Review the rights and responsibilities by asking the group to name a few.

NOTE TO THE LEADER

Emphasize the following concepts:

- It is wrong to touch someone else in a way that takes advantage of another person or is abusive. It is wrong for someone to touch you if you don't want to be touched that way or at that time.
- You do not have to tolerate being touched in any way that makes you feel bad or confused. You can and should decide who touches you and how they can touch you.
- In getting to know yourself in a relationship to another person, either a friendship or love relationship, it can be frustrating to explore what kinds of touch are "good," "bad," or "confusing." It is important to talk about this, to be clear about what are the limits and the preferences you each have.
- Remember, "no" means no and "yes" means yes. Don't get into the "if she says 'no' she means 'yes'" game. Everyone loses. Be as clear and straightforward as you can.

Group Activity:
Make a collage of touching. On a long piece of cardboard, have the group glue pictures from magazines that are examples of good, bad, and confusing touch.

Optional Activities
Story: "Talking Helps" in *No More Secrets For Me,* Oralee Wachter, 1983, Little, Brown & Co. Activity Sheets: 7. "Touches that I Like" 8. "My Very Own Touch Continuum"

Concluding the Session

Summarize and Evaluate
Encourage the group to think about what they learned in this session. What new things did they learn about? What things have they already known about?

Closing
Ask each group member to think of a "good" touch. Explain that they do not need to tell what the "good" touch was, but rather ask the group to share a word that describes how they felt. Words might be "loved," "cared for," etc.

For Your Notebook

John 10:1-10

"Truly, truly, I say to you, anyone who does not enter the sheepfold by the door but climbs in by another way, is a thief and a robber; but the one who enters by the door is the shepherd of the sheep. To this one the gatekeeper opens; the sheep hear the voice of the shepherd who calls them by name and leads them out. After bringing all of them out, the shepherd goes before them, and the sheep follow, for they know the shepherd's voice. A stranger they will not follow, but they will flee away, for they do not know the voice of strangers." This figure Jesus used with the disciples, but they did not understand what he was saying to them.

So Jesus said again, "Truly, truly, I say to you, I am the door of the sheep. All who came before me are thieves and robbers; but the sheep did not heed them. I am the door; whoever enters by me will be saved and will go in and out and find pasture. The thief comes only to steal and kill and destroy; I came that they may have life, and have it abundantly."

[I-LL]

ACTIVITY SHEET 7

Touches I Like

ACTIVITY SHEET 8

My Own Touch Continuum

Think of examples of good, confusing, and bad touch. Put your own examples on the line where they fit.

_____

"GOOD"   "CONFUSING"   "BAD"

(Permission is given to reproduce this page for students.)

Session 6

God Cares About Us

Objectives

- To increase participants' knowledge about "good," "bad," and "confusing" touch.
- To increase participants' knowledge about acquaintance rape or sexual abuse (bad touch) by someone who is not a stranger.
- To practice ways participants can discourage a potential abuser from initiating abusive behavior.
- To increase participants' knowledge that God is sensitive to human suffering, but God doesn't control people's behavior.

Theological and Biblical Concepts

Psalm 13 is a beautiful lament that expresses the feelings of someone who has been a victim. Like many individual laments, it raises difficult questions about why a compassionate God allows people to suffer and why God doesn't take the pain away. Bernhard W. Anderson, in his book *Out of the Depths, The Psalms Speak for Us Today* (pp. 81–82), outlines this Psalm in three parts. Verses 1–2 raise the questions about suffering. Verses 3–4 petition God for deliverance from the enemy. The concluding verses (5–6) are an expression of trust in God's faithfulness.

It is important to note that Psalm 13 (and other laments found in the psalms) is not written out of a lack of belief in God. Rather, it is written by one who has experienced deep suffering and is still motivated by a belief that God listens to one's prayers and petitions. This is a God that is sensitive to the suffering of humans and a God that listens to our prayers. Throughout the centuries, this Psalm has reassured people who have suffered that they are not alone. Others have suffered as they have, and God cares about them.

Resources Needed

Newsprint and markers, or chalkboard and chalk
Bibles
Copies of **FOR YOUR NOTEBOOK,** page 64

This Session in Brief

Getting Started (5 minutes)
Build Community
Questions and Answers

Developing the Session
Expand Safety Rules (5 minutes)
Not Just Strangers (5 minutes)
Demonstration (10 minutes)
Discussion (25 minutes)

Concluding the Session (10 minutes)
Summarize and Evaluate
Closing

Session Plan

Getting Started

Build Community
Ask one member of the group to explain the collage from the previous session. Encourage the group to talk about any pictures that they are not sure should have been placed in their present position. Follow up on the collage by reviewing briefly the touch continuum from Session 5. Stress that each person experiences touch differently.

Questions and Answers
Check the question box for any questions. Ask the group if they have any questions from last session that they want to ask.

Developing the Session

Expand Safety Rules

- Review the list of safety rules listed in Session 4. Use the newsprint from Session 4.
- Remind the group that most of the rules have to do with what a child should do to protect him or herself from strangers.

Not Just Strangers Abuse Children
Explain to the group that most cases of sexual abuse involve someone that the child knows.

- Make a list of people the group knows.
- Ask "Can any of these people harm you in this way?"

Emphasize that an abuser could be a parent or step-parent, an older kid, an uncle, a babysitter, a childcare provider, a teacher, a minister, or anyone else that they know. Therefore, in order to protect children, we need to make rules that help children protect themselves from someone they know.

Add to the newsprint list some rules that the group can think of that might be helpful to remember if someone they know tries to touch them in ways that make them feel bad. Some examples might include:

> Don't do anything that makes you feel bad.
> Trust your feelings.

Remind the group that it is very important that they begin thinking that the abuser could be a stranger, but it could also be someone known to the child.

NOTE TO THE LEADER

The demonstration should be led carefully by the group leader(s). If you are the only group leader, invite another adult to assist you. Several strategies are given for responses to the situation. The first response is less assertive than the second response. The adult leaders should play all the roles in the first response. Do not involve young people in acting out the less assertive response. The group members should never be asked to act out the victim role; rather they should practice the more assertive response. The more assertive response can be repeated several times with different group members playing the role of the child.

Background for the Leader

It is important that the adult leader(s) take time to do both the demonstrations and the role-plays. Each demonstration and role-play is designed to help the group members learn. In particular, role-plays and demonstrations:

1. help children understand feelings and motives of the characters,
2. help the group members practice the skills,
3. help the group members develop empathy for the victim, and
4. help group members see alternative solutions to problems.

Demonstrate Potential Abuse Situations
Demonstrate a potential abuse situation that might be faced by a child. Go through each demonstration once, with the potential victim (adult) playing a less assertive role. Discuss problem-solving in the group, and repeat the situation, with the potential victim (child) being more assertive and getting out of the situation. Discuss how effective each technique would be. What are different responses that a victim might choose? What are some factors that might make one response a wiser response than others? Be sure that the group focuses on realistic options.

Demonstration
The potential victim (male or female) is asked by a babysitter (male or female) to play a game where he or she is supposed to take off his or her clothes. This is a new experience for the potential victim. The babysitter tries different ways to get the child to cooperate, including bribery ("You can stay up late to watch a special show that is after your bedtime") and threats ("I'll tell your parents that you were really bad and that you should be punished.")

A response: The child is clearly uncomfortable and makes excuses for why he or she cannot participate in the game. In the end, the child agrees to play the game.

A more assertive response: The child says to the babysitter, "I don't want to play a game like that. I want you to leave me alone." The child tells his or her parents when they return home.

NOTE TO LEADER

After demonstrations, role-plays, or other forms of participation, the adult leader should affirm persons and the ideas they shared. The affirmation can be for either the individual or the whole group. Some examples include: "Some good ways and ideas shared today were . . ." or "Thank you for sharing. . . ."

Discussion: The child is not to blame

- Explain that sometimes, no matter what the child does, he or she can not escape being touched in harmful ways.
- Stress that it is never the child's fault that the child was abused.
- How might the child feel who has been hurt? Most children will understand that it is very embarrassing for the victim.
- What will happen if the victim does not tell? Explain that usually the abuser will continue to abuse children unless the victim tells someone what happened.

Explain that God loves each child no matter what happens to them. God will always love us. God also gives each of us the promise that God will not leave us.

Why Doesn't God Protect Children?

Read and discuss Psalm 13 (see **FOR YOUR NOTEBOOK**). Look over the materials in the Theological and Biblical Concepts section. Some points to emphasize include:

- People throughout the centuries have experienced suffering, and it often helps us when we have suffered to hear the words written by someone else who has suffered too.
- God is a compassionate God who is concerned and involved with people.
- Even though God does not want people to suffer, some people do bad things to others.
- Child sexual abuse is an example of some of the bad things that happen to children. Even though we know that God cares about children and their safety, sometimes child sexual abuse takes place.
- It is hard for us to understand why God doesn't stop the abuse. But the only way for abuse to stop is for people to stop the abuse.
- God uses people, their minds, hearts, and wills to help each other.

When abuse does happen

Although God can't magically stop the abuse, God is able to help children. Other people are able to stop the abuse. What are some ways that God can help?

- God gives us the courage to say "No!"
- God gives us the strength to tell someone.
- God gives us information to help us protect ourselves and others.
- God gives us comfort when we hurt.

Optional Activities

Story: "Just in Case," in *No More Secrets,* by Oralee Wachter, (Boston: Little Brown and Co., 1982).

Concluding the Session

Summarize and Evaluate
Ask the group, "If you were telling someone about this session, what would you say?" Briefly summarize the learning of this session.

Closing
Read Psalm 13 again prayerfully.

Tell the group that the session will close with prayer. Ask the group members what they would like to pray for. Ideas might include: courage, strength, information, friends, family, comfort, etc.

Prayer
O God, our God, there is so much we don't understand about our world. We don't understand why people get hurt or why bad things happen. We don't understand why people hurt children.

Today we pray for many things. We have named out loud many of the things that we ask for. We ask for strength and courage. We ask for trusted friends and caring adults. We ask for _____ (use ideas from the group's list). We also pray for those who have been hurt by others. May you comfort them and help them to feel your love. Amen.

NOTE TO THE LEADER

When closing with prayer, the group leader or one of the children can read the prayer. As a leader, listen carefully to suggestions from the group about what they would like to pray for. These will give you clues as to what the group is really thinking about.

64

For Your Notebook

Psalm 13

How long, O GOD? Will you forget me forever?
   How long will you hide your face from me?
How long must I bear pain in my soul,
   and have sorrow in my heart all the day?
How long shall my enemy be exalted over me?
Consider and answer me, O SOVEREIGN my God;
   lighten my eyes, lest I sleep the sleep of death;
lest my enemy say, "I have prevailed over you";
   lest my foes rejoice because I am shaken.
But I have trusted in your steadfast love;
   my heart shall rejoice in your salvation.
I will sing to GOD,
   because God has dealt bountifully with me.

[I-LL]

Session 7

What About the Family?

Objectives

- To increase participants' knowledge about incestuous abuse.
- To encourage victims of incest to seek help and potential victims to respond assertively to potentially abusive situations.
- To understand the rights and responsibilities of following the commandment of honoring one's father and mother.

Theological and Biblical Concepts

Historically, biblical material has helped pass values from one generation to another. In almost all churches, the ten commandments are used to teach children basic values. Unfortunately, some of this material has been misappropriated to give people justification to abuse children. In particular, the fifth commandment, "Honor your father and your mother" (Exodus 20:12), has been used to condone treating children as objects rather than treating them as people with both rights and responsibilities.

"Honor your father and your mother" is a straightforward commandment demanding the respect of parents. Although the commandment is most often quoted to children, the commandment is one of ten commandments written primarily for adults. The Hebrew word *kabod,* which has been translated as "honor," means "to take seriously." All too often it is forgotten that the major thrust of the commandment is to instruct adults on the care and respect that should be given to elderly parents within the community of faith.

Ephesians 6:1–4 repeats the commandment found in Exodus. It includes information about the responsibilities of parents. Verse 4 states, "Parents, do not provoke your children to anger, but bring them up in the guidance and instruction of the Sovereign." (*Inclusive-Language Lectionary*) This text emphasizes the responsibilities of both parent and child.

Most importantly, while respecting one's parents, a person still has the right to say "No!" to being abused. The fifth commandment is not a license to abuse and hurt children.

Resources Needed

Newprint and markers, or chalkboard and chalk
3″ x 5″ cards
Bibles
Copies of Activity Sheet 9
Copies of **FOR YOUR NOTEBOOK,** page 72

This Session in Brief

Getting Started (5 minutes)
  Build Community
  Questions and Answers

Developing the Session (50 minutes)
  Understanding Touch by Family Members
  Defining Incestuous Abuse
  Demonstrations
  Discussion
  Bible Study

Concluding the Session (5 minutes)
  Summarize and Evaluate
  Closing

Session Plan

Getting Started

Build Community
Ask the group for key ideas that they have learned during the last six sessions. Review briefly these ideas.

Questions and Answers
Answer any questions that were left in the question box and give the group a chance to ask any new questions about past or upcoming sessions.

Developing the Session

Review

- Ask the group to list who could be an abuser. Remind the group that an abuser could be anyone. Most likely, an abuser is a man, but some abusers are women. Abusers look just like anyone else. They could be of any race. They could look rich or very poor. An abuser could have any kind of job. An abuser could be a minister, a teacher, a postal carrier, a babysitter, a coach, or anyone.
- Ask the group, "Are there members of a family that could be abusers?" Emphasize that an abuser could be an uncle, a step-father or father, an aunt, an older brother, or someone else in a family.

Understanding Touch by Family Members
Review briefly the touch continuum. Look for examples of "good" touch that describe touching by family members. Look for examples of "bad" touch and "confusing" touch. If no one has any examples of touching by family members, ask the group to think of some examples that fit these categories. Some examples might include:
—a father often watching a daughter change clothing
—an older child taking pictures of a nude brother
—a step-father touching a child's private parts
—a mother or father forcing a child to touch his or her private parts
—an uncle demanding that a child sit on his lap or kiss him inappropriately.

NOTES TO THE LEADER

Incest is defined as sexual intercourse between closely related persons where marriage is legally forbidden. This can and does include consensual relationships between adults, most often brothers and sisters, and consensual relationships among children within a family who are engaging in sexual play and experimentation. Incestuous abuse is a more expanded definition in that it includes any sexual activity or experience imposed on a child that results in emotional, physical, or sexual trauma. The forms of incestuous abuse are diverse; the acts are not always genital and the experience not always a physical one. The father who stations himself outside the window of his daughter's bedroom to watch her dress and undress is abusing his child as much as the father who fondles a daughter's breasts.

Whatever form the abuse takes, the scarring of the child can be deep and lasting. Unlike physical abuse, the damage cannot always be seen, but the scars are there nonetheless. The most devastating result of the imposition of adult sexuality on a child unable to determine the appropriateness of his or her response is the irretrievable loss of the child's inviolability and trust in the adults in his or her life. Sexual abuse is a betrayal of the caretaking responsibility of the adult.

* * *

The adult leader should encourage the group to define incestuous abuse themselves. The definition is provided so that the leader can be sure that the definition is correct. It is important that group members feel that they have generated these definitions themselves.

It is also important that participants be allowed to share stories they have heard. Children ages nine through twelve have detailed stories concerning experiences of friends, plots from movies, and other sources. Their story-telling gives them a chance to share as well as learn the definitions of abuse.

Incestuous abuse is defined as sexual contact or other explicit sexual behavior that an adult family member (or older child) imposes on a child. Most often, it takes place between a parent (father or mother) and a child (daughter or son).

Incestuous Abuse

The adult leader should lead the group in a discussion of incestuous abuse. Ask the group to define incestuous abuse. Write the group's definition and the examples on newsprint or on a chalkboard.

Emphasize the following points:

- Incestuous abuse occurs when a more powerful member of the family is sexual with a less powerful member (child or adolescent).
- It may involve any kind of sexual contact or touching a child's private parts.
- This form of sexual abuse can take place between parent or parental figure (for example, step-parent) or other adult family member (for example, uncle, grandfather) and child.

- It is a form of "bad" touch or "confusing" touch.
- The touch may feel "good," but it leaves the child feeling bad about him or herself.
- It usually starts at an early age for the child and may continue until the child tells someone and asks for help.
- This form of abuse is not uncommon.

Discuss with group members the idea of appropriateness. For example, for a small child hugging may have a very different meaning than for a pre-teen. Touching that may be appropriate at one age may be very inappropriate at another. Remind the group that feelings are clues to when touching is appropriate.

Activity: Game
On 3" x 5" cards, write the following situations. Mix up the cards, and take turns reading the situations aloud. After reading the cards, have group members decide whether the touching is "OK" or "Not OK." Discuss each situation by asking what could make it OK or not OK.
Situations:

- A father stands in the bathroom and watches a daughter shower.
- A mother asks a son for a backrub.
- A mother tickles a baby's feet.
- A brother gives his sister a hug on Christmas.
- A mother asks her son to undress so she can take pictures of him in the nude.
- A step-father touches a daughter's private parts.
- An aunt pats a child on the head.
- A mother gives her son a hug.
- A father gives his daughter a hug.
- An uncle touches a boy's private parts.

NOTES TO THE LEADER

Children between the ages of nine and twelve are especially aware of the changes in appropriateness of touch that they are experiencing. The hugs and kisses of loving parents that felt good and were appreciated at age eight may now be a source of embarrassment. Children at this age understand very well that behavior that at one age is appropriate may not be appropriate at another age.

* * *

The demonstration should be led carefully by the group leader(s). If you are the only group leader, invite another adult to assist you. Several strategies are given for responses to the situation. The first response is less assertive than the second response. Do not involve young people in acting out the less assertive response. The group members should never be asked to act out the victim role; rather they should practice the more assertive response. The more assertive response can be repeated several times with different group members playing the role of the child.

Demonstrate Potential Abuse Situations

Demonstrate two potential situations that might be faced by a child within the family context. Go through each demonstraton once with the potential victim playing a less assertive role. Discuss problem-solving in the group, and repeat the situation with the potential victim being more assertive and getting out of the situation. Discuss how effective each technique would be. What are different responses that a victim might choose? What are some factors that might make one response a wiser response than others? Be sure that the group focuses on realistic options.

Demonstration 1[1]

The potential victim (female or male) goes into the bathroom and starts to undress in order to bathe. Having shut the door behind her (him), the door opens and an older brother comes in and just stands there watching. This has never happened to the younger sibling before.

A response: The child is clearly uncomfortable, but saying nothing, waits for the brother to leave. The older brother does not leave, so the child gets up and leaves the room.

More assertive response: The child says to the older brother, "I don't like you watching me. I want you to leave right now." When he leaves, she (he) locks the door. If he does not leave, she (he) puts on a robe and leaves.

Brain-storm other responses: What other responses could the group imagine? What changes in the situation would have made a difference in the response?

Follow-up: What should the child do next? Who could the boy or girl tell?

Demonstration 2[2]

The potential victim (female) is staying home on a Saturday morning to watch cartoons. Her mother is out grocery shopping and will not be home for a few hours. Her step-father is home alone, sitting in the living room while she watches TV. Her step-father tells her to come over and sit on his lap. She has been sitting on her step-father's lap since she was a child, but now she has become uncomfortable with his behavior. She hesitates. This has happened before, and she knows what to expect. But she sits on his lap and he holds her tight and tries to kiss her. She feels uncomfortable, confused, and frightened.

A response: She is clearly uncomfortable and tries to pull away from him but does not succeed. She tells no one about his sexual advances toward her.

More assertive response: She pulls away, stands up, and says "I don't like you to touch me this way. I want you to stop." She then leaves the room.

Brain-storm other responses: What other responses could the group imagine? What changes in the situation would have made a difference in the responses?

Follow-up: What should the child do next? Who could the girl tell? Remind the group that a child should never lie even when an adult tells him or her to.

NOTE TO THE LEADER[3]

Emphasize that incestuous abuse is not wrong because it is sexual. Rather, it is wrong because it involves one person who is older and/or more powerful taking advantage sexually of a person who is younger and vulnerable. The victim is usually manipulated or coerced, or is too confused to know what to do, and so goes along with the sexual activity, not seeing any alternative.

When the sexual contact takes place between an adult male and a male child, this does not mean that either the abuser is gay or that the child will "become" gay due to the contact. It is not wrong because it is sexual contact between persons of the same gender, but because of the exploitation of children.

Sexual contact per se is not wrong. Any adult taking advantage of a child sexually is behaving irresponsibly and illegally. This is a betrayal of the adult role of protector or caretaker who, misusing authority, coerces the child into sexual activity. The child feels exploited and used by the adult for sexual gratification. The child may be confused by or ambivalent about feeling uncomfortable with the adult's sexual approach. The young person will be especially confused about the difference between sexual activity and affection.

Bible Study—"Honor Your Father and Mother"
Read Exodus 20:12.
Discuss the scripture:
    What is this scripture about?
    Who is the scripture written about?
    Is it written just for children?
Read Ephesians 6:1–4.
Discuss the scripture:
    How is this scripture different from Exodus 20:12?
    What does the text ask children to do?
    What is the responsibility of parents?

Scripture gives us clues about how healthy family relationships are to be. This scripture is about having respect for parents. It is not written only for children, but for people of all ages who have parents. "Honor" means to respect, to listen carefully to parents, and to try to follow parental advice. It does not necessarily mean that a child's rights are gone. It especially doesn't mean that a child's right to say "No!" is taken away.

Discuss respecting your parents.
—What does it mean to respect your parents?
—Name some good ways of showing respect for your parents.

Often, scripture is misinterpreted by people who want to use it to justify their own behavior. Sometimes scripture is used by grown-ups to convince themselves that touching a child sexually is OK. This scripture does not give a father, an uncle, or a mother an excuse to sexually abuse a child.

Review some of the main points of our curriculum to this point (this is a good way for those who may have missed a session to catch up):

- Your body belongs to you.
- Every child has a right to say "No!" to abuse.
- Feelings are clues to tell us about "good" and "bad" touch.
- It is not the victim's fault when abuse takes place.
- Tell a trusted adult or friend in order to stop the abuse.
- *Note:* Sometimes a child's other parent doesn't believe the child, but the child should keep on telling someone until someone does believe.
- Each child is a child of God, and God wants each child to be safe.

Emphasize that incestuous abuse is difficult to stop because the child has to say "No!" to and/or tell on a family member. Most often that family member is someone for whom the child really cares.

Remind the group that a person who abuses a child is not bad. They are doing something bad. The grown-up who is abusing needs to change the way that he or she acts. The child cannot change the grown-up's behavior. The child did not make the grown-up do the behavior. The child has the right to be safe.

Optional Activities

Story: "Promise Not To Tell" in *No More Secrets For Me,* Wachter.

Concluding the Session

Summarize and Evaluate
Ask the group to share some ideas learned and feelings about what happened in the session.

Closing
Ask the group to join together to read the litany on the Activity Sheet 9.

For Your Notebook

Exodus 20:12

"Honor your father and your mother, that your days may be long in the land which the Sovereign your God gives you."

[I-LL]

Ephesians 6:1–4

"Children, obey your parents in the Sovereign, for this is right. 'Honor your father and mother' (this is the first commandment with a promise), 'that it may be well with you and that you may live long on the earth.' Parents, do not provoke your children to anger, but bring them up in the guidance and instruction of the Sovereign."

[I-LL]

(Permission is given to reproduce this page for students.)

ACTIVITY SHEET 9

Litany

First Reader: God loves each of us and wants each of us to be safe.

Second Reader: Families should be a place of safety for children.

Third Reader: But some families behave in ways that hurt children.

All: We pray for all young people around the world.

First Reader: We pray for those who are hurt in war.

Second Reader: We pray for those who are abused by others.

Third Reader: We pray for those who are hurt by people in their own families.

All: Let us be a friend to all those who are hurt, just as God is a friend to all. Amen.

Session 8

Saying "No!"

Objectives

- To practice ways participants can respond to abusive behavior.
- To practice ways participants can stop ongoing abuse in their lives or in the lives of their friends.
- To help participants learn that God empowers us and gives us strength against tremendous odds.

Theological and Biblical Concepts

The Old Testament story of David slaying Goliath (1 Samuel 17) is an empowering story of a child overcoming gigantic odds. The text tells us that Goliath had a height of 6 cubits and a span, or 10 feet. His armor weighed five thousand shekels of bronze, or about 150 pounds. Although we do not know how old David was, we know that he was a youth and that no one believed it possible that such a youth could overcome "the champion of the Philistines."

All people need to be reminded about the possibility of overcoming incredible obstacles. Before battle, David prayed for God to deliver him from his enemy. With God's help, David had the strength to confront Goliath and overcome the enemy.

Resources Needed

Newsprint and markers, or chalkboard and chalk
Film: *No More Secrets*
Bibles
Copies of **FOR YOUR NOTEBOOK** page 79

This Session in Brief

Getting Started (10 minutes)
  Build Community
  Questions and Answers

Developing the Session (40 minutes)
  The Story of David and Goliath
  Film and Discussion
  Teaching Prevention Rules
  Role-play
  Ways that Children Are Tricked

Concluding the Session (10 minutes)
 Summarize and Evaluate
 Closing

Session Plan

Getting Started

Build Community
Describe briefly the plan for the session today. Take a few minutes to ask each group member what they remember from the previous sessions.

Questions and Answers
Check the question box and try to answer any questions that the group has.

Developing the Session

The Story of David and Goliath (see Theological and Biblical Concepts Section)
 Read 1 Samuel 17.
 Discuss the story:

- What happens in this story?
- How does this story of a youth overcoming a giant make you feel?
- Why does David believe that he can overcome Goliath?

NOTE TO THE LEADER

No More Secrets is an excellent film that describes four different situations that children could find themselves in. The group of children, all ages nine through twelve, brain-storm about ways to prevent or stop the abuse in their lives.

The film can be used two different ways:

1. Stop the film at the end of each section and use the time to discuss each situation.
2. Show the whole film and discuss the film.

(This film is so good that it might be advantageous to show it more than once.)

This film can also be a good film to show to parents, perhaps in a special session for them, while the leaders have access to the film. Parents can also discuss the different kinds of abuse and problem-solve how to help the abuse stop.

An alternative activity is to read together the book *No More Secrets.*

The film can be ordered from:
O.D.N. Productions
74 Varick Street
New York, NY 10013
Phone: 212-431-8923

Activity: Film *No More Secrets* and Discussion

- How was the relationship among the kids special?
- How did that relationship help each kid deal with his or her life situation?
- Name the abuse that happened in each situation.
- Are there other options that each kid could have used?
- How could each person be helped by a friend?
- How could the church help any of the kids in this group of friends?

What to do when someone tries to hurt you

Have the group make a *new* list of how to protect themselves. Write this list either on newsprint or chalkboard. Be sure that the following items are emphasized:

- Trust your feelings.
- Stay away from someone when you think that person might hurt you.
- Say "No!" (This does not always work, but try it anyway.)
- Tell a trusted adult

Role-play or Puppet Play

1. Read the following background story.

"Margaret and Mark were twins. They had an older sister and a younger brother. The twins' parents were away bowling, and their older sister was out on a date. Although their brother was already in bed, they were allowed to stay up an extra hour because they were older. Both twins were sitting on the couch when the babysitter (a male) asked them if they liked boys and girls.

"Margaret and Mark didn't know what to tell the babysitter. Their friends at school were both boys and girls. The babysitter asked them if they had ever seen a man without any clothes on. The babysitter then showed them some pictures of naked people. After that, the babysitter took off his clothes.

"When the twins were finally allowed to go to bed, they both felt really embarrassed and confused. Margaret decided to talk to Mark about what happened. Mark was thinking that they could talk to their older sister. Maybe she could tell them what to do."

2. Ask three group members to play Margaret, Mark, and their older sister Marjorie. (If there are children in your class with those names, be sure to substitute other names.) Place three chairs in the front of the room. Tell Marjorie that she is to be as helpful as she can. Ask the group to think about what they would say in Marjorie's place.

3. After the trio has tried some dialogue, ask the class for other suggestions about what would help the twins and statements that may make it worse. (Helpful—believe them, be serious, help them to tell a trusted adult. Unhelpful—laugh, tell everyone else at school, tell them that they should have enjoyed it, act embarrassed.)

4. Brain-storm about what to do if Marjorie had not been helpful. What should the twins have done next? Who else could they talk to?

NOTE TO THE LEADER

Role-playing can be a terrific way to practice skills learned in these sessions. This particular role-play's objective is to practice and increase awareness of peer support of persons victimized by sexual assault.

Successful role-play depends on many different things. Pay special attention to the following points:

- Make the atmosphere relaxed.
- USE ONLY VOLUNTEERS; NEVER ASK A CHILD TO PARTICIPATE.
- Use leaders to fill extra roles if needed.
- Never ask a child to play the role of a victim; rather the role-playing should be an empowering experience in which the child learns about possible options to prevent or stop the abuse.

If the group has never role-played, use a simpler situation or a demonstration first. Then ask the group to do a more complicated situation.

For younger, less mature groups, or groups that do not respond to role-playing, use puppets for the children to act out the situation. Another alternative is to talk out the situation as a group, but practicing telling others is an important aspect of prevention.

For more role-plays, see Plummer, *Preventing Sexual Abuse,* pp. 68–74.

Ways that Children are Tricked
Ask the group what ideas they have about how a grown-up or older child might try to trick a child. List examples of each.

1. *Bribe*—"I'll give you some money for video games." "I'll buy you a new bike." "I'll let you ride my horse anytime you want."
2. *Threats*—"I'll tell everyone that you did it anyway." "I'll kill your pet." "Something just might happen to your parents." "I won't let you play with your friends ever again."
3. *Confuse*—"It will feel good, don't be scared." "Everyone does things like this." "We'll make it our little secret." "You are bad and deserve to be punished." "I need you to do this for me." "Your parent was hit by a car. Come with me to the hospital."

One More Look at Our List
Take the list of rules that the group wrote on newsprint at the beginning of this session. Review it and add any additional ideas that the group has after seeing the film and role-play.

Optional Activities

Story: "What If," in *No More Secrets.*
Bible Study:
   Read and discuss some other story of people of great courage.
   Ruth—Ruth 1:7–14
   Deborah—Judges 4

Concluding the Session

Summarize and Evaluate
Spend a few minutes recalling what has happened during the session. Answer any questions about this session and give the group some ideas about what will happen in future sessions.

Closing

As in Session 2, close this session with a quiet period of relaxation and silence. Finish with a prayer.

Ask each group member to find a place to lie down. (It would be a good idea to provide towels or sheets of paper for each member of the group.) Explain that the group will have a few minutes of silence. Remind the group to breathe deeply. Deep breathing is important if group members are to feel comfortable. During this time, we will be thinking about change.

Explain that the questions asked are not to be answered out loud; rather they serve to give each person something to think about.

Are you breathing deeply? How does that breathing make you feel?
Do you have your eyes open or closed?
When you close your eyes, does it make you feel more alone?
Can you feel your heart beating?
Is your heart beating fast, slowly, or in between?
You can slow it down somewhat by breathing, in and out, . . in and out. . . .

Think of a situation that you want to change in your life. . .
—a relationship with someone that you don't like
—a bully that bothers you at school
—a friend that tells your secrets.

What are some of the possible ways that you can change this situation? Think of as many ways as you can.
Are there any new ways that you can think of after today's session?
Are there friends or adults that you can talk to about this situation?
Think of the next step you should take to change this situation.

As the group comes back together, ask them to pray together the prayer on the **FOR YOUR NOTEBOOK,** page 79.

For Your Notebook

O God, we thank you for ways to help us make changes in our lives. We know that changing situations is not easy. We pray for courage and strength to make changes. We ask for help from others, our friends or trusted adults. Give us the power to keep on telling until change takes place. Help us to be strong like David so we can do the right thing. Amen.

(Permission is given to reproduce this page for students.)

Session 9

No More Secrets

Objectives

- To explore ways to tell a trusted adult about abuse.
- To explore ways to help a friend who has experienced sexual abuse.
- To provide participants with information about local resources available to victims of assault.
- To increase participants' awareness that we experience the love of God through the help and presence of others.

Theological and Biblical Concepts

In Matthew 25:31–40, Jesus tells the disciples a parable of the last judgment. The Ruler divides the people into two groups. According to the Ruler, one group is blessed, and will inherit the realm. The Ruler tells this group that they inherit because of their behavior. They have fed, clothed, and cared for the Ruler. The group questions the Ruler, "When were you hungry, and I fed you?" The Ruler answers that when you help someone else, you are helping the Ruler. When you receive help, you experience the love of God through the help and presence of others.

This parable describes a group of people who are blessed because of their caring for others. In this wonderfully direct way, Jesus charges each of us to become a caring community. To show our love of God, we reach out to others in need.

Therefore, the people of God are a community that cares about others. This community makes up the church. The people of God and the church are a resource for those in need. The church may be a place where trusted adults can help a victim. In addition, each person in the group, as a person of God, can be a friend to others. If each person has some idea about what to do when someone comes to them for help, each person can be a better friend. Helping others is a way to express our love of God.

Resources Needed

Newsprint and markers, or chalkboard and chalk
Pamphlets and brochures from local agencies
Copies of Activity Sheet 10 and **FOR YOUR NOTEBOOK,** pages 86

This Session in Brief

Getting started (10 minutes)
Build Community
Questions and Answers

Developing the Session (40 minutes)
Review Prevention
Bible Study
Who Can you Tell?
Help a Friend
Local Resources
It's Not Your Fault

Concluding the Session (10 minutes)
Summarize and Evaluate
Closing

Session Plan

Getting Started

Build Community
Ask the group what they remember as the most important points in the last session.

Questions and Answers
Ask if anyone has any questions and check the question box.

Developing the Session

Review Prevention
Briefly go over the newsprint from the last session about what to do if someone tries to hurt a child.

Bible Study
Read Matthew 25:31–40 (see **FOR YOUR NOTEBOOK**).
Discuss the scripture reading (see Theological and Biblical Concepts Section).
—Jesus told many parables; can you retell the story he told?
—In the parable, who do you think the Ruler is?
—In the parable, who do you think the people are?
—According to the parable, why is the group on the right hand blessed? What did they do that was so good? What was Jesus trying to tell us that we should do? What are the specific helping actions we are asked to do to show our love of God?

Discussion: Who can you tell?
On newsprint, make a list of all the people that the group can think of who could be trusted to talk to about sexual abuse if it happened to them or someone they know. The group may be reluctant to use names of people. Therefore, people can be identified by their role or job. The list could include:

a special teacher,
the school nurse,
a parent,
a grandparent,
a church school teacher.

Remind the group that each person's list would be different because each of us feels close to different people. Each of us would feel more comfortable talking to special people in our lives.

Ask the group what a person should do if the person that they choose to talk to doesn't believe them. Explain that sometimes grown-ups think that the child is making up the story.

Activity: Hand out Activity Sheet 10. Give each group member a few minutes to complete the exercise.

NOTE TO THE LEADER

Role-playing is an excellent way to learn skills. Use the role-playing as an opportunity for the group to learn prevention skills in a safe environment. Remember that role-playing is not practicing for a play; rather it is practicing skills. Remember:

- Introduce the activity as "pretending." This pretending is skill-practicing.
- Do not comment on the child's performance as an actor. Any evaluation should concern the child's use of information and skills.
- Give lots of positive reinforcement. Acting and answering questions about role-playing can be frightening, and children may need lots of encouragement and reinforcement that they are doing fine.
- USE ONLY VOLUNTEERS FOR ROLE-PLAYS. Do not draft group members, recognizing that sexual abuse may be a current concern for some of the children.

Let's Pretend: Role-play[1]
1. Read the following background story.

"Brenda has an uncle named John. She really likes her uncle, but lately Uncle John has been acting differently. Sometimes he stares at her. He tells her dirty stories and tries to rub her between her legs."

2. Ask the group to list people whom Brenda could tell. Ask four group members to play some of these people. Try to include two adult characters and two children. Assign a character to each of the four group members. Instruct two of them to be helpful to Brenda and two to be either too embarrassed or afraid to help her, or perhaps not even believe her. Try to give these instructions in writing or out of the earshot of the rest of the class.

3. Ask someone to play Brenda. Ask her to try to tell these people about her Uncle John. After she has attempted to tell, you may ask the class to suggest what Brenda should do next. It's encouraging to arrange it so that the last person Brenda tells is the most helpful.

NOTES TO THE LEADER

Often the first person that a child tells about ongoing abuse is a trusted friend their own age. Therefore, it is essential that prevention training include teaching children about what to do if a friend discloses abuse. The abused child may have no one that he or she trusts, but a trusted friend may be influential in getting help.

* * *

After demonstrations, role-plays, or other forms of participation, the adult leader should affirm persons and ideas. The affirmation can be for either the individual or the whole group. Some examples include: "Some good ways and ideas shared today were. . ." or "Thank you for sharing. . . ."

What can we do to help a friend who is being hurt or has been hurt?
Review what should be done for a friend if a friend comes to talk to someone from this group.

- Listen.
- Talk.
- Show you care.
- Tell your friend to tell an adult who can help.
- Go with your friend to tell an adult.
- Give the friend suggestions about who could be trusted.
- Give the friend information about where to get help.

Ask the group how they might feel when a friend might tell them about being hurt. Examples of situations might include being abused on a trip, being the victim of advances by an older teenager, or being abused by a family member. Some of the feelings might include:

- embarrassed
- strange
- uncomfortable
- nervous
- disbelieving.

Explain that very often when a child is being sexually abused, he or she doesn't really trust anyone. It might be important that a member of this group could bring the friend to someone that they trust.

What happens to me and my family if I tell?
In order to stop someone from hurting children, it is essential that the crime be reported. That is the only way that the grown-up who is hurting children can be helped.

- Explain that in some cases the police need to be called.
- Sometimes child protective services needs to be called.
- It may be important that a doctor be called or that the child be taken to a hospital to make sure he or she is OK.

Emphasize that there are many reasons why a child might be afraid. A child might worry that the family will be separated or that someone he or she cares about might go to jail. Sometimes a child has been threatened, and the child thinks that the abuser will carry out those threats.

The most important thing is that the child will be safe. The grown-ups will try to be as helpful as they can to stop the hurting.

Local Resources

Tell the group that there are a variety of agencies and resources locally that can help them if someone hurts them. Discuss each resource with the group.

NOTE TO THE LEADER

Before this session, phone some local agencies: child abuse councils, child protective services, or other agencies. The agencies will have brochures or pamphlets, cards, and lists of other resources. It is important that every church have a list of social agencies and referral numbers for child abuse, rape crisis, women's shelters, and other related issues.

It's not your fault

Finally, reinforce the idea that no matter what happens to a child, God loves each one. It is never the child's fault if something bad or hurtful happens to him or her. Sometimes a child may have broken a parental rule, like going someplace where they shouldn't have, but this is not a reason for a child to blame him or herself.

Explain to the group that we would like to believe that the church is a safe place for children, but sometimes it isn't. However, we hope that the church is a place where there are some trusted adults who care about children. The community of the church is a place where each of us can grow and heal. We can experience the love of God through the caring of people.

Concluding the Session

Summarize and Evaluate

Ask the group for comments and questions that they might have concerning the topic or this course. Assure them that you will be available to them if they want to talk more about any of the topics in this class or just to talk.

Closing

As in Session 8, close this session with a quiet period of relaxation and silence. Finish with a prayer.

Ask each group member to find a place to lie down. (It would be a good idea to provide towels or sheets of paper for each member of the group.) Explain that the group will have a few minutes of silence. Remind the group to breathe deeply. Deep breathing is important if group members are to feel comfortable. During this time, we will be thinking about change.

Explain that the questions asked are not to be answered out loud; rather they serve to give each person something to think about.

Are you breathing deeply? How does that breathing make you feel?
Do you have your eyes open or closed?
When you close your eyes, does it make you feel more alone?
Can you feel your heart beating?
Is your heart beating fast, slowly, or in between?
Think of a person whom you love and trust.

    —a teacher

    —a minister

    —a church school teacher

    —a parent

    —the school principal

    —a friend

Now think of one question that has been bothering you. It could be a question about something that has happened to you. Or it could be a question about advice that you need from someone.

    Imagine that you are going to talk to this trusted person.

        Where were would you meet this person?

        How would it feel to talk to this person?

    Imagine what you would say.

    Imagine what he or she would say.

        How does it feel to talk to this person?

Ask the group to come back together and sing the song from Session 4.

FOR YOUR NOTEBOOK

Matthew 25:31–40

When the Human One comes in glory, with all the angels, then that one will sit on a glorious throne. All the nations will be gathered before the Human One, who will separate them one from another as a shepherd separates the sheep from the goats, placing the sheep on the right, but the goats on the left. Then the Ruler will say to those on the right, "Come, O blessed of [God], . . . inherit the realm prepared for you from the foundation of the world, for I was hungry and you gave me food, I was thirsty and you gave me drink, I was a stranger and you welcomed me, I was naked and you clothed me, I was sick and you visited me, I was in prison and you came to me." Then the righteous will answer, "Sovereign, when did we see you hungry and feed you, or thirsty and give you drink? And when did we see you a stranger and welcome you, or naked and clothe you? And when did we see you sick or in prison and visit you?" And the Ruler will answer them, "Truly, I say to you, as you did it to one of the least of these my sisters and brothers, you did it to me."

[I-LL]

(Permission is given to reproduce this page for students.)

ACTIVITY SHEET 10
"WHO CAN I TALK TO?"

A TEACHER OR COUNSELOR,
A MINISTER OR FRIEND

(Permission is given to reproduce this page for students.)

Session 10

Justice And Forgiveness: Responding to Harm

Objectives

- To clarify for participants the meaning of forgiveness and to relieve them of an obligation to forgive in a vacuum.
- To help participants identify and affirm their need for justice before forgiveness is possible.

Theological and Biblical Concepts

In Jesus' sermon to the disciples in Luke 17:2–3, Jesus tells us that justice and forgiveness are interrelated ideas. Jesus reminds the disciples of the importance of justice. Before someone can be forgiven, he/she must repent. The words, "I am sorry. It will never, ever happen again," are crucial to forgiveness, but they are not sufficient. Action must accompany these words.

All too often, victims of abuse and violence are told that they must immediately forgive the offender. Even when the offender denies the abuse and often is continuing to abuse other victims, our culture, particularly Christians and churches, pressures victims to forgive.

Resources Needed

Copies of **FOR YOUR NOTEBOOK,** page 93

This Session in Brief

Getting Started (10 minutes)
   Build Community

Developing the Session
   Bible Study (15 minutes)
   Story and Discussion (25 minutes)

Concluding the Session (10 minutes)
   Summarize and Evaluate
   Closing

Session Plan

Getting Started

Before the session, pick two pictures, without words, that show a person (perhaps a child) getting hurt. One picture should be a picture of hurt that comes from an accident (car accident, bicycle accident, etc.). Another should be a picture of hurt that comes from intention (a bully picking on another kid, some example of violence, etc.).

- Show the group both pictures.
- Ask the group to make up a story about how each hurt happened.
- Talk about the differences.
—How do the people feel in each picture?
—How are the injuries different?
—How are the people affected?
- How does the intentional wrong we receive make us feel?
- What do we call those wrongs or hurts that are done on purpose?

Developing the Session

Bible Study

- Read Luke 17:2–3 (see **FOR YOUR NOTEBOOK**).
- Ask the participants to talk about what they think forgiveness means.
- Remind the group that sometimes the anger and hurt can be so deep that it is difficult to forgive.

Story
Read the following story. Pause to ask the questions that follow sections of the story.

"Once there was a girl named Suzanne. She was ten years old. She lived in the city [or the country] with her Mom and Dad and her two older brothers. Suzanne liked to ride her bicycle all around; she loved to go swimming at the local pool; she always helped her mother work in the garden raising flowers and vegetables for the family. Suzanne's whole family went to church regularly. Her father taught Sunday school and her mother sang in the choir.

"When summer came and school was out, Suzanne's cousin came to stay with her family. He was sixteen years old and very tall. Suzanne remembered that he had visited them once before when she was very young. But this time he was to stay the entire summer. He got a job working at the corner gas station. Suzanne liked him because he would play catch with her in the backyard.

"One day when he came home from work, he found Suzanne weeding the garden. No one else was home. He called her to come into the house, saying that he needed her to help him. Suzanne went in immediately. He asked her to come into the basement and hold something for him while he hammered it together. When they got downstairs, he grabbed her arm and twisted it. She cried out but there was no one to hear her. He told her that he wanted her to touch him. She didn't understand what he meant. He began to take his pants off. He made her rub his private parts."

How do you think Suzanne felt?

Suzanne was scared. She knew he had tricked her, but she didn't know what to do, so she did what he said. After about ten minutes, her cousin started to put his pants back on. He grabbed her other arm and twisted it. He made her promise that she wouldn't tell anyone about this. He said that if she told, he would kill her cat. She didn't tell.

What would you have done?

_____

NOTE TO THE LEADER

During the discussion, carefully notice responses from the children that would blame or hold Suzanne responsible; for example, "she should have just run away." Follow up blaming statements with additional questions, so that participants understand that there may have been nothing else that Suzanne could have done at the time. For example, respond by saying, "Do you think she could have run away?"

_____

"A week later, her cousin waited until no one else was at home, and he took Suzanne into the basement again. This time he made her take her clothes off and he rubbed her private parts. Again he threatened her and made her feel scared.

"But Suzanne decided that she would go to her mother. She knew that her mother would know what to do and would protect her from her cousin.

"Her mother was shocked at Suzanne's story, but she believed everything Suzanne said. She called the Sexual Abuse Center and asked for their help. When Suzanne's father got home, her mother told him, and together they talked with her cousin. He denied everything. He said that Suzanne always made up stories, that she had asked him to take his pants off.

"They were very angry with her cousin. They told him that he would have to go and talk with the police and the counselor at the Sexual Abuse Center. They made certain that Suzanne was never left alone with him again. They contacted his parents, Suzanne's aunt and uncle, and told them what had happened."

How do you think Suzanne felt? (Possible responses may include: grateful, embarrassed, still scared.)

"Suzanne told her best friend, Molly, what had happened. Molly was very surprised, but she also believed Suzanne and stood by her. Molly told Suzanne that the Bible said she should forgive her cousin, that if she was really a good Christian, she would want to forgive him and be his friend. Molly said that would make everything fine again."

If Suzanne followed Molly's advice, do you think everything would have been fine now?

How do you think Suzanne felt about this talk with Molly?
(Possible responses may include: confused, upset, angry, relieved, obligated, guilty, etc.)

Do you think she felt like forgiving her cousin at this point?

"Suzanne did not like to hear Molly say this. Suzanne still felt angry about what her cousin had done to her.

"Suzanne's cousin had to appear in court. Suzanne went to court with her parents and told her story there. Her parents reminded her that this was not her fault. Her cousin now admitted what he had done, but he made it sound like it was really Suzanne's fault. Even though he said he was sorry, Suzanne could tell he didn't really mean it. The judge said that her cousin was guilty of child molesting; that it was very wrong; that he should never have done these things to Suzanne. Then the judge ordered her cousin to go to counseling for three years.

"Several months later, Suzanne began to think about what Molly had said about forgiveness. She still felt guilty because she hadn't forgiven her cousin. So she went to her minister for a talk. Her minister, whose name was Kathy, listened to her story. Pastor Kathy told Suzanne how sorry she was that all of this had happened to her. Suzanne asked if she had to forgive her cousin for what he did. Pastor Kathy said she didn't have to forgive him until she was ready. Forgiveness, she explained, is a gift that God gives us to help us heal from painful experiences. It is a way to be able to move past the painful memories and get on with our lives.

"Pastor Kathy reminded Suzanne of the time that she had been playing with her older brother and he accidentally hit her in the head with a hoe. The hoe cut her head and it bled, so her father took her to the doctor to have the wound stitched up. Her brother went along and held her hand. He told her how sorry he was to have hurt her. He said that he should have been more careful and that he would never play that way again.

"Pastor Kathy asked Suzanne to look in the mirror. Did she see the scar that was left from the cut? She answered yes. Does she think about this painful event every day? No, said Suzanne; only when I see the scar. Had she forgiven her brother for hurting her? Yes, said Suzanne. But he was sorry for what he did.

"That's right, said Pastor Kathy. He was sorry and he also took responsibility for being careless. Because he did those things, you were ready to forgive him. And that has meant that you put that whole experience behind you and hardly ever think about it any more.

"We need some things to happen before we are ready to forgive. We call these things justice. We need the people around us who love us to support us when we are hurt and scared. We need our parents and other adults to help us and protect us. We need the person who hurt us to take responsibility, to apologize, to promise never to hurt a child again. You will know when you are ready to forgive, said Pastor Kathy. When you are ready, God will help you and will put the memories of your molestation in the back of your mind so you won't think of them very often. Then you can continue to grow into a young woman who will always know that she is loved by God and by her family and friends."

How do you think Suzanne felt now?

Continued Discussion:
Ask participants to think of a time that someone their own age did something that hurt them.

- How did they feel?
- Did they automatically forgive that person?
- Did they ever forgive that person?

Ask participants to think of a time when someone older than they did something that hurt them.

- How did they feel?
- Did they automatically forgive that person?
- Did they ever forgive that person?

More Bible Study

Read Luke 17:2–3 again.

Jesus makes it clear in this passage that anyone who harms a child is in very deep trouble. And when Jesus instructs us what to do, he begins with the need to *rebuke* a person who harms children. This means that some adults need to confront that person and stop him or her from harming other children. Then he says that if the person *repents,* we should forgive him or her. To repent means to take responsibility for having hurt someone and to never, ever do it again. This means making big changes. In order to make these changes, people who hurt children need help. Only then can we be ready to forgive.

NOTE TO THE LEADER

Be careful not to reinforce a child's sense of obligation to forgive harm done to them in the absence of repentance and justice.

Concluding the Session

Summarize and Evaluate
Ask the group members to shut their eyes and think of words that were important to them today.

Share the words you feel comfortable sharing.

Closing
Read Psalm 119:76.

> "Let your constant love comfort me,
> as you have promised me, your servant."

[TEV]

We hope that each one experiences the church as a place of healing. We sing. We pray. We work together as sisters and brothers in God's family. When we sit together in church, God helps us think, through quietness and hymns, scriptures, prayers, and sermons.

For Your Notebook

Luke 17:2–3

"It would be better for him if a millstone were hung round his neck and he were cast into the sea, than that he should cause one of these little ones to stumble. Take heed to yourselves; if your brother sins, rebuke him, and if he repents, forgive him. . . ."

[RSV]

(Permission is given to reproduce this page for students.)

Session 11

Peer Pressure

Objectives

- To increase participants' understanding of peer pressure and how it can encourage abusive behavior.
- To increase participants' understanding of stereotyping and how stereotypes can impact relationships and can support abuse.
- To increase participants' understanding that our faith can give us strength to do what we think is right even when we experience peer pressure.

Theological and Biblical Concepts

The band of people who followed Jesus from place to place probably was much larger at times than just the twelve disciples. Certainly the number of disciples decreased at times to even a few persons. Together, Jesus' disciples experienced peer pressure. They understood what it was like to be part of a group.

John 6:60–69 tells of a time when the message that Jesus brought was particularly difficult for his followers, and many of the followers left Jesus. The Revised Standard Version Bible says that Jesus' message was a "hard saying," meaning offensive or difficult. The twelve disciples had difficult decisions about whether they would continue to follow Jesus.

Jesus asked the twelve if they too would go away [v. 67]. Verses 68–69 contain Peter's decision to stay with Jesus, "the Holy One of God." Peter probably experienced the pressure to go with the others who found Jesus' message difficult.

This story of Peter reflects the experience in which pre-teens and teens often find themselves. The pressure of joining the group influences people of all ages. Taking responsibility for what an individual believes is right is hard, but our faith empowers us to stand up for what we believe is right.

Resources Needed

Magazines
Paper, scissors, glue
Newsprint and markers, or chalkboard and chalk
Copies of **ACTIVITY SHEET 11** and **FOR YOUR NOTEBOOK,** page 98

This Session in Brief

Getting Started (5 minutes)
  Building Community

Developing the Session
  Bible Study (10 minutes)
  Discussion of Peer Pressure (5 minutes)
  Identify Expectations in Relationships (10 minutes)
  Activity: Collages (20 minutes)
  Discussion (5 minutes)

Concluding the Session (5 minutes)
  Summarize and Evaluate
  Closing

Session Plan

Getting Started

Building Community
Begin the session with community building. In order to reconnect the group, ask:

- What is the main thing you recall from the last session?
- Are there any questions or comments about last session?

Developing the Session

Bible Study
Ask the group to read John 6:60–69 (see **FOR YOUR NOTEBOOK**). Look over the material in the Theological and Biblical Concepts section. Some points to emphasize include:

- Jesus, the disciples, and many other men and women followers worked and traveled together. They were a close group of friends who knew each other well.
- Toward the end of Jesus' ministry, many of the followers left Jesus.
- How do you think Peter felt as many people started to leave Jesus?
- Why did Peter decide to stay with Jesus?
- Like Peter, our faith helps us have the courage to do what we believe is right regardless of what others do.
- Pressure from our friends to do something or not to do something is called "peer pressure."

Discuss Peer Pressure
Peter probably felt pressured to leave Jesus as the other followers were doing. The pressure from friends and others to be like them can sometimes encourage us to do things we wouldn't otherwise do. Discuss with the group:

- What is peer pressure?
- Give examples of situations where you have felt peer pressure.
- What happens if you go against your friends?

Identify Expectations in Relationships[1]
1. Separate the group into male and female (if you have a male and female leader). In each group, ask members to list on newsprint what kinds of things they want:
—in a friend of the same sex
—in a friend of the opposite sex
—in a romantic friend or date.
   2. Look at the responses in each of the three categories. Discuss the lists in terms of differences and similarities.
   3. Discuss: Why are the lists different?

NOTE TO THE LEADER

Emphasize the importance of a range of personal qualities in any friend rather than relying on just looks and possessions. Judging a person or being judged on these things alone may result in inaccurate expectations, which could lead to an abusive situation. For example, not all long-haired, sloppy men are mass murderers. Likewise, not all clean-cut men are nice, warm, caring people.

Bring the group back together. Post all lists and compare responses from the female group and the male group. Ask girls to comment on the boys' list and boys to comment on the girls' list. This often leads to some direct challenges between boys and girls, which result in helpful clarification of their expectations of each other. For example, the boys might say, "Girls want to be cheerleaders." Or the girls might say, "All boys love sports."

NOTE TO THE LEADER

Young people may have some inaccurate perceptions and expectations of each other that need to be challenged. The leader should carefully allow the group to confront expectations that they think are incorrect. Frequently, a group will be so homogeneous that all the boys and girls agree on expectations. Therefore, it is important that the adult leader raise questions that challenge those expectations that do not value persons as children of God.

Discussion
Peer pressure affects how we use stereotypes and often forces people to adopt stereotypes. Remind the group that often a group decides what is good or bad about another group. When we don't judge people individually, but rather by a group to which they belong or by the way they dress, we are stereotyping.

Define Stereotypes [2]
Discuss stereotypes.

- Ask the group, in general, what is a stereotype? Define a stereotype as a commonly held image of or belief about people or things as a group, usually not based on fact or reality; that is, the image or belief is often false.
- Ask participants for examples of stereotypes. List these on the board or newsprint.
  For example, all blonde females are dumb; all football players have a low IQ; all German Shepherd dogs are vicious and dangerous; men are always stronger than women; a person who wears a straggly beard and dirty clothes is dangerous.

Collage Activity
Ask each group member to make a collage on a piece of paper (8½" x 11") that will fit into the book that each group member is making. Ask each group member to select pictures that together make a picture of what each person thinks an ideal friend (boy or girl) would look like.

- How would the person look? What color hair? How would this person dress?
- Are there ways to picture what a person is really like?
- What kinds of things would this person like to do?
- Are there ways to picture what kind of a friend someone is?

Discussion
While the group members work on cutting pictures and making this collage, use the time to talk about stereotypes.

- What images do we have for a "sexy" person?
- How can you tell that someone would make a good date?
- At school, can you tell by looking at a person whom you would someday like to date?
- How do you tell which people you meet would make good friends?
- How do you tell which people you meet would make a good date?
- Are there different groups at school, and can you tell who is in the different groups by how these people dress or act?
- How do you show others that you are an individual?

During the discussion, point out that teenagers, especially, have stereotypes.

- How are these stereotypes helpful?
- How can these stereotypes hurt?
- What stereotypes are found in the group members' collages?

Concluding the Session

Summarize and Evaluate
Share group members' collages. Talk abut some ideas learned and feelings about what happened in this session.

Preparing for the Next Session
Bring in an advertisement that shows stereotypes of males and/or females used to sell a product.

Closing
Read together the litany on Activity Sheet 11.
  Pray the prayer together.

For Your Notebook

Many of the disciples, when they heard it, said, "This is a hard saying; who can listen to it?" But Jesus, knowing that the disciples murmured at it, said to them, "Do you take offense at this? Then what if you were to see the Human One ascending back into heaven? It is the spirit that gives life, the flesh is of no avail; the words that I have spoken to you are spirit and life. But there are some of you that do not believe." For Jesus knew from the first who those were that did not believe, and who it was that would betray him. And Jesus said, "This is why I told you that no one can come to me unless it is granted by [God]. . . ."

After this many of the disciples drew back and no longer went about with him. Jesus said to the twelve, "Do you also wish to go away?" Simon Peter answered him "To whom shall we go? You have the words of eternal life; and we have believed, and have come to know, that you are the Holy One of God."

[I-LL]

(Permission is given to reproduce this page for students.)

ACTIVITY SHEET 11

Leader: The disciples were part of a group who followed Jesus.

People: But each disciple was also an individual person.

Leader: Peter had to decide for himself whether he would stay with Jesus or leave as did the others.

People: Others, such as Mary Magdalene, also decided to stay with Jesus to the very end.

Leader: We are all part of groups. We have family and friends that we care about. It is fun to be part of the group and be with others.

People: But we are also individual persons. Sometimes we disagree with our friends or families. We have to decide for ourselves what we want to do.

Leader: Often we make judgments about people because of the way they look. We place value on special clothes or possessions.

People: We are reminded that we must look beyond how a person dresses, or what they own. We must look at what kind of a person they are.

Prayer: O God, we are reminded that you love us and care about our safety. Help us to be aware of pressure that is put on us by our friends or others around us. Sometimes this pressure convinces us to do things that we don't want to or to say things that we don't believe.

Give us strength, O God, to say and do what we think is right.

O God, we also know that we often judge people by the way they look, the things they own, the color of their skin, or whether they are a boy or a girl. But you, O God, judge us by the kind of person that we are.

Forgive us, O God, when we judge people by the stereotypes that we have. Give us the wisdom to see beyond outward appearances. Amen.

Session 12

Advertising/Males and Females in Media

Objectives

- To increase participants' awareness of the representation of men and/or women as sex objects, and of violence used in both advertising and media imagery as sources of stereotypes and values about women, men, and relationships.
- To increase participants' willingness to accept responsibility for making decisions about their lives.

Theological and Biblical Concepts

The creation story in Genesis 1:26-31 makes it clear that we are all created in God's image. This is a difficult concept, because we each have various images of God. Some of us think of God as loving and caring. Others think of God as fearsome and terrible. Although we may not all agree, there are some qualities that we can all agree on.

During this session, the group will be asked to think about what they imagine God to be like. With God's qualities before us, we can think better about what it means to be created in the image of the Creator. In addition, how does this image compare with the image that the media gives us of what we should be like?

Resources Needed

VCR
Tape with sample videos and advertisements
Newsprint and markers, chalkboard and chalk

This Session in Brief

Getting Started (10 minutes)
 Building Community
 Questions and Answers

Developing the Session (50 minutes)
Brain-storming stereotypes
Discussion
Bible Study and Talk about Images
Take Action

Concluding the Session (5 minutes)
Summarize and Evaluate
Closing

Session Plan

Getting Started

Building Community
Ask each group member to think about what his or her life will be like in five years. (Most group members will be in high school within five years.) Ask each member to share about the following:

- Who will be their friends?
- What will be their favorite hobby?
- Will they be dating?

Developing the Session[1]

Ask the group to brain-storm a list of all the ways we learn stereotypes that affect our behavior, such as: TV, videos, movies, songs, stories, jokes, books, schools, churches. Then ask, what are some of the messages we get from these sources about sexual assault? For example: It's cool. Women really want to have sex, even when they say "no." Boys will be boys. Violence is sexy.

Images in Media
Show the tape of various videos and ads.

NOTE TO THE LEADER

Although not all churches own a VCR, it is important that the group be able to look at videos critically. Access to a VCR can be obtained by renting a machine or by having this session meet in someone's home. Before the session, rent or tape videos and ads from television.

Concerning the video taping off-the-air of materials and copyright laws, it is important that the group leaders understand that videotaping off-the-air for instructional use in church school class falls into an uncertain area of the copyright laws. One-time copying of parts of programs for face-to-face instruction in the classroom, where attendance is limited to teacher and pupils, the purpose is instruction and not entertainment, and the showing is part of the teaching activities of a non-profit educational institution, is permitted. However, no one seems to know if church school classes are included in this definition. "The Video Copyright Guidelines" can be obtained for $1 per copy from the Presbyterian Church (USA), 100 Witherspoon St., Louisville, KY 40202-1396.

Discuss[2]

- Which ads and videos are most familiar? Can you give other examples of ads or videos that illustrate stereotypes?
- What are the values expressed by these ads? Ask the group to identify characteristics of a "Real Man" and a "Real Woman" according to advertisements. List on newsprint or chalkboard. For example:

Real Man	Real Woman
muscles	young
pumping iron	diet
aggressive	stylish hair
strong	slim
tough	jazzercise
never smiles	passive
moustache	never wears glasses
in control	sexy

- Whom do you know who "measures up" to the advertising image?

Bible Study

Read Genesis 1:26-31 again (see Session 1, **FOR YOUR NOTEBOOK**). On a piece of newsprint, brain-storm about what qualities we imagine God to have. Some answers might include: loving, caring, always present.

Discuss what being made in God's image means:

- What image does God have of us?
- What responsibility do we have if we are made in God's image?
- What qualities does each of us have that are similar to qualities of God?
- Do we have to dress a certain way because we are created in God's image?

NOTE TO THE LEADER

Most children think about God as a person. This activity of listing the qualities of God is a good place to emphasize that God is personal, but not a person. The qualities of God should include qualities that culturally are thought of as both male and female. The list should also include qualities that could be found in everyone.

Talk about Advertisements[3]

Ask the group members to share with the group the advertisement they brought in and to explain how it stereotypes women or men or how it uses an abusive or violent image. Have some current magazines available in case someone forgot to bring in an ad.

NOTE TO THE LEADER

The images we are sold in advertising and the images that pre-teens watch daily on TV videos are unreal, glamorized, and impossible to achieve even if we wanted to. Yet these are powerful images that do affect us and make us feel inadequate if we do not successfully fit the image. The images of the ways that men and women relate also shape our expectations about our own relationships.

Take action[4]
Discuss with the group what can be done about offensive advertising and videos. Here are some suggestions:

- When you see an ad or video, stop and think about what image or fantasy is being sold to you and evaluate how you feel about it.
- Think for yourself. Then say to yourself: "I don't like this." "I don't believe this." This gives us a way to gain some distance from the message and not be so easily taken in by it so that we will automatically buy the product the next time we are in a store.
- Talk to your parents or another adult about how you feel, and think about this particular situation involving offensive advertising.
- Register a complaint. Call or write the magazine, radio, or TV station. Ask your parent or another adult to go with you into a store with an abusive window display and tell the manager how you feel about it. For example: "I find your advertisement for this album to be abusive and sick. I'm not going to buy any more albums here until you stop advertising this way."

NOTE TO THE LEADER

Advertising, as well as visual images in TV videos, which stereotypes men and women and uses abusive images, contributes to the problem of sexual and physical abuse by saying it's OK, glamorous, and sexy.

These images affect us all. If it didn't work, they wouldn't use it.

Sexual and physical abuse are not isolated problems but occur in a larger context. Prevention of the problem requires addressing the root causes, for example, advertising that glamorizes, stereotypes, and abuses.

Concluding the Session

Summarize and Evaluate
Ask group members what was new information for them in this session. Ask them: Do you have any further questions about the effects of advertising and how it relates to stereotyping and sexual abuse? Are there any questions about TV videos? Do you have any questions from any part of the course? Is there any additional information you would like to have?

Closing

Write a group poem. Ask the group for three summary words. Have each group member write one line about each of the three words on a 3″ × 5″ card. (Group members do not need to sign their names.)

On newsprint, write the three words. After collecting the cards, write all the sentences to make a poem. Read the finished poem to the group.

NOTE TO THE LEADER

This poem makes a great addition to the notebook that each group member is making. Type out the poem and duplicate it for the next session. For an additional activity, ask group members to illustrate the group poem.

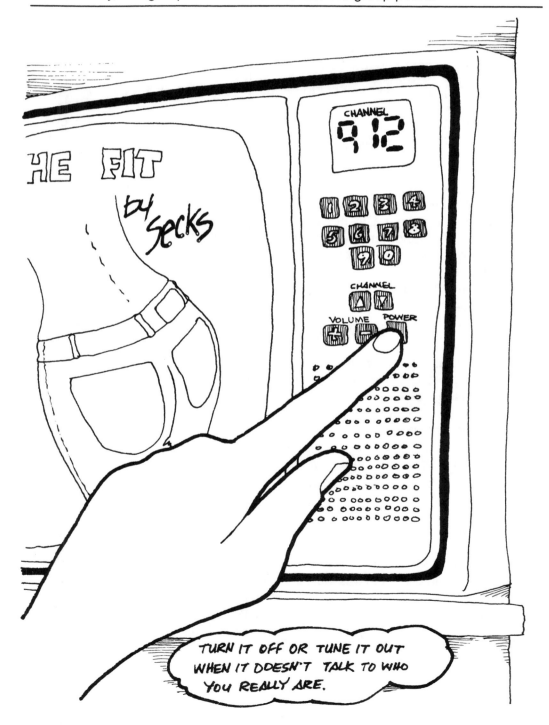

Session 13

Wrapping It Up with a Positive Self-Image

Objectives

- To review the major concepts of the series of sessions.
- To bring closure to the group's experience.
- To reinforce participants' understanding that God loves each group member.

Theological and Biblical Concepts

In the book of Isaiah, the prophet reminds us of how precious each of us is to God (Isaiah 43:1-4a). The scripture is written to tell the people of Israel how much God cares about them.

In 587 Before Current Era (BCE), the country of Israel had been conquered by the Babylonians, and many of the people had been taken as prisoners to live in Babylonia. The people were allowed to return to their native land in 539 BCE. They were afraid that perhaps after so many years of living in this foreign land, God did not love them anymore. In this scripture, Isaiah told the people that not only did God love them, but God was calling them to come back to their homes. Even though this scripture was written a long time ago, the message also applies to us. A basic tenet of our Christian faith is that each person is of infinite worth. The Bible reminds us that God loves us and will always be with us. When tragedy and bad things happen to us, God comforts us and helps us heal. The people of God are a resource to help us.

Resources Needed

Copies of **FOR YOUR NOTEBOOK,** page 108
Supplies for creating a book out of all the activity sheets.
FOR YOUR NOTEBOOK, and any other materials that have been collected during the past sessions.
Poster board (or heavy newsprint) and markers
Masking tape
Cassette tape or record of quiet, meditative music
Cassette tape player or record player

This Session in Brief

Getting Started (10 minutes)
   Building Community

Developing the Session
   Bible Study (10 minutes)
   Activity: Our Books (10 minutes)
   Brain-storming (10 minutes)
   Creating a Poster Walk (10 minutes)

Concluding the Session (10 minutes)
   Closing—Poster Walk

Session Plan

Getting Started

Building Community
Remind the group that this is the last session. However, the leaders will still be available for any questions the group members have or any help that they need.

Developing the Session

Bible Study

- Read Isaiah 43:1-4a (see **FOR YOUR NOTEBOOK**).
- Give the group some historical background of the passage. Use the Theological and Biblical Concepts section to give you the important information.
- Discuss the passage:
    How might the people of Israel have felt about returning home?
    Can you think of a time when you were worried that your family or a friend might not love you anymore?
    Can you think of a time when you were worried that God might not love you anymore?
    How do you think the people felt when they heard this message about God's love?

Activity: Our Books
During the past sessions, the group members have been collecting Activity Sheets, **FOR YOUR NOTEBOOK** pages, collages, and other materials to include in their books. In this last session, all materials should be collected so that each group member can take their books home.

Brain-storming about the Sessions
Ask the group to name the major learnings of this series of sessions. On newsprint or a chalkboard, list the major topics. Major topics should include:

- I am a child of God.
- My body belongs to me.

- My feelings are part of God's creation.
- My feelings are clues about what is happening to me.
- I can say "No!"
- God will comfort me.
- No one has the right to touch me and make me feel bad.
- God cares about the suffering of people.
- I have rights and responsibilities.
- I have learned ways to protect myself.
- God gives me strength.
- I can talk to a trusted adult.
- The church can be a place to go for help.
- People who have hurt someone should be sorry for hurting others.
- Just because others do something, it doesn't mean it is right for me.
- God loves me.

NOTE TO THE LEADER

This activity is meant to encourage the group to respond to the whole series of sessions. This review should also be personal. Encourage group members to use their own words to name these topics. Add any topics that the group misses. This activity is also an excellent way to evaluate the sessions. The leaders should be able to tell which topics the group remembers and which topics had the greatest impact on the group members.

Creating a Poster Walk

- Explain that the group will be making a poster for each major topic. (The group may have to decide which ideas are the most important, because the number of participants in the group will limit the number of posters.)
- Ask each group member to choose one idea listed during the brainstorming activity. (Remind the group that not everyone will get their first choice, as each idea should have a group member to make a poster.)
- Using newsprint and markers, ask each group member to make a poster that illustrates the idea.
- Ask group members to spread out, so each person can work alone.

Concluding the Session

Closing—Poster Walk

- Hang the posters in the same order as the ideas appeared in the sessions.
- Play quiet music.
- Ask group members to take a slow, non-verbal walk, looking at each person's poster and remembering the idea that the poster represents. Give each person a few minutes at each poster.
- Begin the walk by reading this prayer:
    "God help me to be still. Help me be quiet and listen to you."
- Sing together the song "I am a Promise."
- Read together the scripture from Isaiah 43.

For Your Notebook

Isaiah 43:1-3a, 4a

But now thus says the Lord, who created you, O Jacob, who formed you, O Israel:
"Fear not, for I have redeemed you;
    I have called you by name, you are mine.
When you pass through the waters I will be with you;
    and through the rivers, they shall not overwhelm you;
when you walk through fire you shall not be burned,
    and the flame shall not consume you,
For I am the Lord your God,
    the Holy One of Israel, your Savior. . . .
Because you are precious in my eyes,
    and honored, and I love you. . . ."

[RSV]

(Permission is given to reproduce this page for students.)

Appendix A

Sexual Abuse Fact Sheet

- Child sexual abuse is when someone is forced or tricked into sexual contact. This includes obscene phone calls, fondling, intercourse, anal or oral sex, prostitution, and pornography.
- Incestuous parents love their children but put their sexual/intimacy needs before those of their children. Sometimes this is due to a crisis period in their lives or because boundaries in the family get confused or unclear.
- The average victim of child sexual abuse is between eight and eleven years old.
- Some experts estimate that five or six children in a typical classroom of thirty have been affected by sexual abuse, regardless of geographic area, race, or socioeconomic class.
- Ninety to ninety-seven percent of abusers are men, at least in cases presently reported.
- Between 60 and 90 percent of victims of child sexual abuse are girls.
- Offenders are *not* usually strangers to children. Seventy to eighty percent of offenders are known to children.
- Fifty percent of child victims are molested in their own home or in the offender's home.
- Heterosexual males present greater risk to boys and girls than homosexual males.
- The average length of an incestuous relationship is three years; it is rarely a one-time occurrence.
- The victim may cope in many ways: by being either withdrawn, delinquent, or an overachiever in school. Victims of sexual abuse are typically not as involved with their peers as other children.

(Permission is given to reproduce this page for students.)

Appendix B

Indicators of Sexual Abuse in Children

The following physical and behavioral characteristics may signal that a child is a victim of sexual abuse. As with other lists of symptoms, some of the same signs may indicate other types of problems. Until recently, sexual abuse was not often considered as a possible reason for erratic or problem behavior. It is important to recognize that sexual abuse is a possibility when a child/adolescent exhibits several of the following behaviors.

Physical Signs:
Bruising, bleeding, or infections in the genital/anal area. Physical symptoms may be manifested as difficulty in walking, sitting, or urinating; scratching or tugging at clothing around the genital area; torn, stained, or bloody clothing; genito-urinary complaints or infections.

There may be no physical indicators that a child is being abused.

Behavioral/Attitudinal Signs:

- Eating, sleeping, and eliminating disturbances
- Recurrent physical complaints
- Withdrawn or aggressive behavior
- Tired, lethargic, sleepy appearance
- Fearful or suspicious of adults
- Sexually explicit language or behavior not appropriate to the child's age.
- Regressive behavior such as whining, excessive crying, thumbsucking, wetting, or soiling self
- Aversion to a particular person, place, or situation
- Change in school performance, truancy
- Fear, worry, overly serious, depressed
- Anger toward or dislike of adults, authority figures
- Running away from home
- Suicide threats or attempts
- Behavioral defiance, sexual promiscuity, prostitution
- Shy, withdrawn, overburdened appearance
- Substance abuse that is more than experimental
- Reluctance to undress for physical education
- Stealing, shoplifting
- Pregnancy wishes
- Interest in early marriage
- Attraction to older men or dislike of men
- Excessive hand washing, bathing
- Unreasonably restricted social activities or overly protective father
- Poor self-image, low self-esteem

- Fantasies about victimization or violence
- Alienation from family members, rejection of typical family affection
- Fear or strange men and/or strange situations
- Fear of being alone
- Overly clinging or dependent behavior
- Extreme avoidance of touch
- Abrupt change in behavior or personality
- Extreme overachiever

APPENDIX C

How to Help a Child Victim of Sexual Abuse

Anytime during the teaching of this unit, a group member may disclose that he or she has either experienced sexual abuse or is presently experiencing ongoing abuse. The first reaction of an adult to whom a child discloses is very important.

Many adults' first instinct is to ask questions so as to find out whether the experience is true or untrue. It is essential that this task be left for the professionals.

Here are helpful suggestions for responding to a victim's disclosure:

1. Listen carefully to the child's recounting of his or her experience. This is a time to be loving and supportive.
2. Tell the child that you believe that he or she is telling you the truth. Reassure the child that what has happened is not his or her fault.
3. Thank the child for sharing with you and make it clear that you are very sorry that this has happened to him or her.
4. Explain that you will do everything that you can do to make the abuse stop. In order to help him or her, you must tell other people who can help.

Above all, make it clear that you will stand with the child. Make it clear that you will do everything you can do to be supportive.

APPENDIX D

Reporting Child Sexual Abuse

Teachers often feel confused about what circumstances and with what procedures sexual abuse should be reported. Although we feel confused, the question should not be *if* we should report (legally and morally we are required to), but rather *how* to report. Find out about your church policy, which may have standard guidelines as to whom and how the formal report should be made.

When to Report

In all states, we as teachers, parents, administrators, nurses, social workers, and concerned citizens must legally report any suspicion of child sexual abuse. Fortunately, we do *not* need to investigate the reality of that suspicion. Protective Services of the Department of Public Welfare is legally mandated to do such an investigation. We should also keep in mind that according to federal legislation, (Public Act 93-247, January 31, 1974), each state must "have in effect a state child abuse and neglect law which includes provision for immunity for persons reporting . . . from prosecution . . ." and that the report will be kept confidential.

Guidelines for reporting are:

1. Whenever children tell you that they have had sexual contact with an adult (person over eighteen years old).
   a. intercourse
   b. fondling or touching
   c. anal or oral sex
   d. used sexually in photographs, films, or video
2. Whenever children tell you they have been forced or tricked into sexual conduct with another child. (Particularly a child five or more years older, or a child sixteen to eighteen years old.)
3. Whenever friends or acquaintances of a suspected victim report to you that the child has reported such abuse to them.
4. When physical evidence of sexual abuse is discovered (physical harm or irritation in genital areas or VD).

BE AWARE of the following indications that sexual abuse may have been or may be going on:

1. Sudden change in mood or personality
2. Sudden change in school performance
3. Extreme withdrawal from social contacts with peers
4. Acting out behaviors—fighting, exhibitionism, drug usage, runaways
5. Seductive behaviors—learned from being used sexually
6. Aversion to touch or closeness/listlessness
7. Psychosomatic illnesses

8. Unusually fearful and distrustful of adults
9. Overly compliant in attempts to please adults
10. Lying or stealing.

How to Report

If you have questions about reporting or need additional information, contact your Child Protective Services Unit, Department of Public Welfare. Please report situations as soon as possible to facilitate services to children and families. Report *even if* the child states the abuse has ended or that they have already told someone about it. Protective Services' trained staff will do the investigation.

Your local Child Protective Service number is ———————————————.

Appendix E

What Happens When a Report is Made

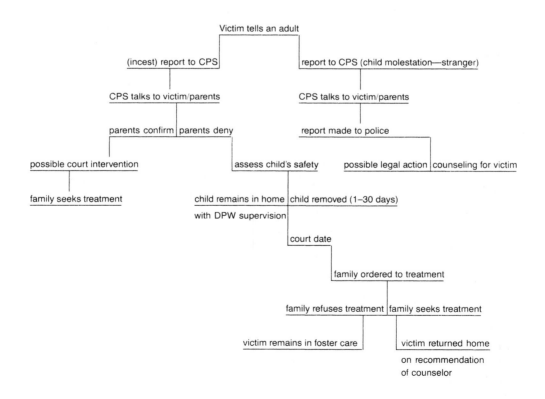

Appendix F

Reporting Child Abuse: An Ethical Mandate for Ministry

by Marie M. Fortune

The epidemic problem of child abuse in the United States (physical, sexual, and emotional) presents persons in ministry with a challenge and an opportunity. When child abuse is disclosed, the religious leader can intervene with sensitivity and compassion to bring an end to this suffering, which has most likely been chronic. Yet intervention by a minister is not necessarily forthcoming because of hesitancy, confusion, lack of information, and ambivalence. Situations of child abuse are complex, and a minister may well try a private solution and avoid using other community resources, usually to the detriment of the child and the family.

An Ethical Mandate

The ethical mandate for Christian ministry in response to the abused child is rooted in Jesus' gospel teachings. In Matthew, Jesus points to the child as the one who is the greatest in the kingdom:

> Whoever receives one such child in my name receives me; but whoever causes one of these little ones who believe in me to stumble, it would be better for him to have a great millstone fastened round his neck and to be drowned in the depth of the sea (Matt. 18:5–6, RSV).

Jesus is consistent in his assertion of the specialness and value of children in a cultural context that regarded children as property of their father. He also points clearly to the responsibility of those around children to care for them. This teaching must have been consistent with Jesus' understanding of the Hebrew custom of hospitality, in which the orphan, widow, and sojourner were identified as being the responsibility of the entire community, which was to provide for their needs and protect them. What is at stake here is these persons' vulnerability, which is a consequence of their life circumstance. Children are by definition vulnerable and in need of care and protection by adults. When this care and protection are not provided by adults, and when those whose responsibility it is to protect are in fact the source of pain and abuse for the child, then someone else must act to provide for the child. Such is the situation faced by a religious leader to whom it is disclosed that a child may be abused.

Fortune, Marie M. "Reporting Child Abuse: An Ethical Mandate for Ministry," *Abuse and Religion: When Praying Isn't Enough,* Edited by Anne L. Horton and Judith A. Williamson. Lexington Books, D.C. Heath Co., Lexington, MA, 1988.

The other ethical principle that applies here is that of "justice-making" in response to harm done by one person to another. Christian scripture here is very specific: "Take heed to yourselves if your brother sins, rebuke him, and if he repents, forgive him" (Luke 17:3, RSV). The one who harms another must be confronted so that he might seek repentance. Both Hebrew and Christian scriptures are clear that repentance has to do with change: "get yourselves a new heart and a new spirit! . . . so turn and live" (Ezekiel 18:31–32, RSV). The Greek word used for repentance is *metanoia,* "to have another mind." In this context of repentance, accountability, and justice, forgiveness and reconciliation may be possible. These should be the primary concerns of the religious leader.

Final Goals

As with all forms of family violence, child abuse requires an immediate response and a recognition of a larger context. The goals of any effective response should follow this order:

1. Protect the child from further abuse.
2. Stop the abuser's violence.
3. Heal the victim's brokenness and, if possible, restore the family relationships; if not possible, mourn the loss of that relationship.

Taking these steps in order provides the best possible opportunity for eventual restoration of the family. Until the first two goals are successfully accomplished, the third is unachievable. It is certainly possible to have the victim and offender living in the same place and giving the appearance of being an intact family, but unless the victim is safe and the offender has taken steps to stop the abuse, there is no restoration and no intact family.

In situations of child abuse, these goals can best be accomplished by the early reporting of suspected child abuse to legal authorities. Every state in the United States provides a mechanism at the state level for reporting, investigating, and assessing situations where children may be at risk. They also have the professional resources with which to assist victims, abusers, and other family members in addressing the three goals of intervention.

Reporting: Reasons to Report

1. *Facts about child abuse:*

   Offenders will reoffend unless they get specialized treatment.

   Offenders against children minimize, lie, and deny their abusive behavior.

   Offenders rarely follow through on their good intentions or genuine remorse without help from the outside.

   Treatment of offenders is most effective when it is ordered and monitored by the courts.

   The pattern of the abuse must be broken in order to get help to the victim and offender.

   Quick forgiveness of the offender is likely to be "cheap grace" and is unlikely to lead to repentance and change. These factors emphasize the need to use an external, authoritative, specialized resource in order to bring change for the family.

2. *Access to specialized resources for treatment:* Unless the ministers are specially trained to provide treatment for victims and abusers of family violence,

they alone are not an adequate resource to the family. The pastor's role is critical throughout, but the most important first step is reporting.

3. *Access to a means to protect a child and require accountability from an offender:* The child protective service or law enforcement offices in a community are the only bodies authorized to investigate allegations of abuse, provide physical protection for a child, and restrain the behavior of an adult who is abusive.

4. *Deprivatizing the situation:* Involving the services of a community agency requires that the silence which has supported this chronic situation be broken. It is not simply a private, family matter; it is a community concern. The consequences can no longer be avoided. Again, this offers the best chance to provide help to a hurting family.

5. *Setting a norm:* Involvement of the wider community clearly communicates to all involved that the physical, sexual, or emotional abuse or neglect of a child is intolerable because children are important and it is our collective responsibility to protect them.

6. *Mandatory:* In every state, persons in helping professions are mandated to report the suspicion of child abuse to the authorities. In some states, the religious leader is exempt from this requirement. In every state, any citizen *may* report suspected child abuse and not be liable for an unfounded report if the report is made in good faith. With or without a legal mandate, clergy should consider the weight of an ethical mandate to report.

Why Ministers May Hesitate

The ambivalence many ministers feel about reporting child abuse comes at the point when other considerations supersede the fundamental goal of protecting the child. Such things as protecting family privacy or the status of the adults in the family, fears of breaking up the family, or perceptions of the social service providers as punitive or insensitive to the religious beliefs of the family make it difficult for a religious leader to refer or report. Yet once ministers receive a disclosure, they have the authority and responsibility to protect children who cannot protect themselves.

Reporting: How-Tos

Sometimes the hesitancy to report comes from a lack of understanding of what will happen once a report is made. Every state has a statewide agency responsible for child protection.[1] Generally, a report is made to indicate there is suspicion that a child is being harmed. The religious leader need not have specific evidence and need not attempt to gather evidence or detailed information from the person who discloses. If it sounds as if abuse may have occurred and the child is still at risk, then the child protection agency should be notified. It will investigate the situation and assess the risk to the child. In some communities, it will encourage the alleged abuser to temporarily leave the home. Frequently, when there is no other available option, it will remove the child temporarily from the home. If there is evidence of abuse, it will take the case to the prosecutor, who will then decide whether to file charges. Whether charges are filed or not, the child protection agency will offer counseling to the child victim and nonoffending family members. If the abuser is convicted, the court may mandate counseling as an alternative to prison time. Adults seldom serve time for child abuse convictions.

Problems and Suggestions

Another cause for hesitation in the religious leader is the fear that reporting will be perceived by abusers as turning them in and thus will damage, perhaps irrevocably, the pastoral relationship. Two factors mitigate against this fear. First, it is seldom the abuser who discloses; it is most likely the child/teenage victim or the nonoffending family member who calls for help. Second, the way in which the report is made significantly shapes the perception of the person who has disclosed.

For example, if a religious leader conveys any ambivalence to someone at the first hint of abuse by saying "Don't tell me any more or I will have to report this," the context is set for a punitive and secretive situation. The minister is also withholding possible assistance from the person who is seeking help. Further, it is not helpful for the minister to listen to a disclosure, never indicating that a report must be made, then wait until the person leaves to call and report anonymously. This may relieve the conscience, but does not help create a context in which the religious leader can continue to minister as a part of wider intervention.

Instead, it is helpful when hearing a disclosure to indicate that additional help will be needed in order to aid the victim, save the family, help the abuser, and so forth, and that the best resource to begin with is the child protection service. Suggest that the person who has disclosed call the agency with you present, and offer to be with them when the social service provider comes to talk with them. Help the person disclosing to understand that the child protection worker can provide much more in addition to what you can do and reassure the discloser that you will not desert him or her. Then seek to work *with* the child protective service worker to provide for the needs of the members of the family seeking help.

What to Expect With Disclosure/Reporting

Offenders will frequently be the last people you would expect to sexually molest a child. They may well be highly regarded, upstanding citizens who are active in the congregation. Do not allow your impression of these people in public settings to prevent you from entertaining the possibility that they may have molested a child.

Initially, the offender will usually deny all responsibility and will seek to discredit the victim's story by attacking its credibility: "She lies about everything, but this is the most ridiculous one she's told yet." It is always tempting to believe the adult's denial because our society has never taken children's words very seriously.

Very rarely do victims falsely report an offense. If they have summoned the courage to tell someone about their situation, they almost always have been harmed by someone. Victims may also quickly recant their story because they feel extreme pressure from family members and maybe even the offender to do so. Their recantation does not mean the abuse did not occur or that this person is now safe. Nonoffending family members (usually mothers) initially may not believe their child, but instead feel pressure to support the offender against the child. The mother may also be a victim of spouse abuse.

When a report is made to the legal authorities, chaos usually erupts. The whole family is in crisis. It may take several weeks for this very complex situation to be sorted out. The results of disclosure and reporting may not be a final resolution to the incestuous abuse situation in a family, but some attention to this matter is better than none.

Special Considerations

Confessions and Confidentiality

Many people in pastoral roles perceive a contradiction between their obligation to preserve confidentiality of communication with a congregant and their obligation to report the suspicion of child abuse. They see this contradiction as a conflict of ethical demands. Part of the perceived conflict arises from the interpretation of confidentiality and its purpose, particularly as it rests within the responsibility of the religious professional. The context for an analysis of these ethical demands is the understanding of confidentiality that comes to the religious professional from multiple sources.

The purpose of confidentiality has been to provide a safe place for a congregant or client to share concerns, questions, or burdens without fear of disclosure. It provides a context of respect and trust, within which help can hopefully be provided for an individual. It has meant that some people have come forward seeking help who might not otherwise have done so out of fear of punishment or embarrassment. Confidentiality has traditionally been the ethical responsibility of the professional within a professional relationship and is generally assumed to be operative even if a specific request has not been made by the congregant or client.

For the minister, unlike the secular helping professional, confidentiality rests in the context of spiritual issues and expectations. In Christian denominations, the expectations of confidentiality lie most specifically within the experience of confession. The responsibility of the pastor or priest ranges from a strict understanding to a more flexible one—from the letter to the spirit of the law. For example, for Anglican and Roman Catholic priests, the confessional occasion with a penitent person is sacramental; whatever information is revealed is held in confidence by the seal of confession, with no exceptions.[2] The United Methodist *Book of Discipline* does not view confession as sacramental but states, "Ministers . . . are charged to maintain all confidences inviolate, including confessional confidences."[3] The Lutheran Church in America protects the confidence of the parishioner and allows for the discretion of the pastor: "no minister . . . shall divulge any confidential disclosure given to him in the course of his care of souls or otherwise in his professional capacity, except with the express permission of the person who has confided in him or in order to prevent a crime."[4] Even within Christian denominations, there is a range of interpretations of the expectations of confidentiality which are not necessarily limited to the confessional occasion.

What are Confidentiality and Secrecy?

It may be useful in this discussion to make a distinction between confidentiality and secrecy. Secrecy is the absolute promise never under any circumstance to share any information that comes to a member of the clergy; this is the essence of sacramental confession. But a commitment to secrecy may also support maintaining the secret of child abuse, which likely means that the abuse will continue. Confidentiality means to hold information in trust and to share it with others only in the interest of the person involved, with their permission, in order to seek consultation with another professional. Information may also be shared without violating confidentiality in order to protect others from harm. Confidentiality is intended as a means to help an individual get help for a problem and prevent further harm to herself or others. Confidentiality is not intended to protect abusers from being held accountable for their actions or to keep them from getting the help they need. Shielding them from the consequence of their behavior will likely further endanger their victims and will deny them the repentance they need.

In addition, confidentiality is not intended to protect professionals; it is for those whom they serve. It should not be used as a shield to protect incompetent or negligent colleagues, or to protect them from professional obligations. Thus, confidentiality may be invoked for all the wrong reasons and not truly in the interest of a particular congregant or of society. This was never the intent of this special provision of pastoral communication.

Disclosure within Different Faiths

When a disclosure is made by an offender in a confessional setting, the religious leader has the opportunity to respond within the parameters of a particular faith's tradition while keeping in mind the overriding priority of protecting the child victim. For example, a Roman Catholic priest can hear the confession of a child abuser, prescribe penance to report himself to the child protection service, and withhold absolution until the penance is accomplished. Confession to a priest does not carry with it the priest's obligation to absolve in the absence of penitent acts. Confession opens the opportunity for the penitent persons to repent and to make right the harm they have done to others. Likewise, for a Protestant in a nonsacramental confessional situation, directives may be given and actions prescribed which include the abuser reporting himself to child protection services. If it is clear that the penitent will not follow the directive of the religious leader and self-report, then some Protestant ministers have the option and the obligation to report directly. The vulnerability of the child and the significant likelihood that the abuse will continue supersede an obligation to maintain in confidence the confession of the penitent.

Cooperation: Working with Secular Service Providers

In addition to a long-standing breach between religious and secular professionals concerned with mental health issues, some substantive concerns have often prevented ministers from working effectively with social service providers or therapists. All these concerns come to the fore when the issue of reporting child abuse is raised: separation of church and state, involvement of the criminal justice system, disregard for a family's religious beliefs, and breaking up families. While the state should not interfere with the practice of ministry, it does have the lawful responsibility of protecting children from harm. The church should see this as a common agenda and work with those designated to carry out this mandate. Even with its multitude of shortcomings (not the least of which are sexism and racism), the criminal justice system can provide a mechanism to enforce accountability for offenders and should not be avoided to protect offenders from embarrassment or the serious consequences of their abuse. A family's religious beliefs deserve respect. But any effort by family members to use religious beliefs to justify abuse of a child or deflect intervention intended to stop abuse should be challenged by both religious and secular professionals. Finally, outside intervention to protect a child does not break up the family. The abuse which preceded the intervention broke up the family and endangered its members. Temporary separation of family members may well be the only possible means of healing and restoration, and should be used when appropriate.

Cooperation between religious and secular professionals expands the resources available to a family experiencing abuse. The special skills each can bring are much needed by family members. Religious leaders can concentrate on their pastoral responsibilities in concert with the social service provider, who can guide the intervention and treatment.

Conclusion

Situations of suspected child abuse are seldom simple and straightforward. Religious leaders should be guided by a commitment to the overriding priority of protection of children and by a clear sense of the limits of their own resources. The mechanism of reporting child abuse and the resources that follow from it are invaluable tools for the minister. Clarity of purpose will direct an ethical mandate to use every available means to stop the abuse of a child.

Resources on Sexual Violence

Child Sexual Abuse—A Handbook for Clergy and Church Members, by Lee W. Carlson, Valley Forge: Judson Press, 1988.
   A practical and accessible resource for clergy and lay leaders.

The Child Sexual Abuse Prevention Guidebook, by Cordelia Kent. Sexual Assault Services, Hennepin County Attorney's Office, Minneapolis, MN 19079.
   The concept of "touch continuum" has been further developed through physical (dance and theater) interaction with many groups of children along with materials for teaching by Ms. Kent. Contact her at the Illusion Theater.

Feeling Safe, Feeling Strong: How to Avoid Sexual Abuse and What to Do if It Happens to You, by Susan N. Terkel and Janice E. Rench. Minneapolis: Lerner Publications, 1984.
   Written for children between ages of eight and twelve, this book can be read by a child alone or with a trusted adult. It includes seven stories that describe situations of children in sexual abuse. The specific topics are personal rights, pornography, exhibitionism, incest, obscene phone calls, and rape. The book emphasizes problem-solving.

The Educator's Guide to Preventing Child Sexual Abuse, edited by Mary Nelson and Kay Clark. Santa Cruz, CA: Network Publications, 1986.
   This collection of essays inform the reader of many different aspects concerning the prevention of child sexual abuse. Topics include: children as sex objects, what happens to victims, the role of the teacher, and contemporary theories and their applications.

He Told Me Not to Tell, by Jennifer Fay. King County Rape Relief, 1025 South 3rd St., Renton, WA 98055.
   This book is a guide for talking to children about sexual assault. Information encourages parents to use correct body part names, back up their children when they say "No!", and ways to identify assault victims.

No More Secrets For Me, by Oralee Wachter. Boston and Toronto: Little, Brown and Company, 1982.
   A book for children to read alone or with a trusted adult, it tells about four different children whose rights have been abused and what they did in their situations.

Preventing Sexual Abuse: Activities and Strategies for Those Working with Children and Adolescents, by Carol A. Plummer. Holmes Beach, FL: Learning Publications, Inc., 1984.
   This curriculum is written for school teachers and counselors. It contains a skeleton outline of a program for teaching prevention techniques. It also includes games and activities.

Private Zone, by Frances S. Dayee. New York: Warner Community Co., 1982.
Written for children from three to nine with an adult interpreter, the book focuses on "private zones" and who should touch a child. It explains that children have the right to say "No!" and to tell another adult when inappropriate touching occurs.

Sexual Abuse Prevention Education: An Annotated Bibliography, compiled by Kay Clark. Santa Cruz, Ca: Network Publications, 1985.
This inclusive bibliography details most books and films for adults, children, and youth in the area of sexual abuse prevention. It also lists film distributors. It is an essential listing for educators.

Sexual Violence: The Unmentionable Sin, by Marie M. Fortune. New York: The Pilgrim Press, 1983.
In this ground-breaking book, the author leads the reader through a carefully spelled out argument, first defining her subject matter—explaining how even the words "sexual violence" have been explained away from the perspective of the offender—and concluding with a thesis that can hardly be disputed: Sexual violence undermines all levels of social well-being, and must be stopped. She also explores how the confusion arises between sexuality and sexual violence, explaining the difficult nature of consent.

Films

No More Secrets, O. D. N. Productions, 74 Varick St., New York, NY 10013.
This film is about four friends, ages eight through ten, who share their experiences of abuse. The film emphasizes problem-solving and telling a trusted adult to prevent or stop the abuse.

Notes

Introduction

1. Diana E.H. Russell, "The Incidence of Prevalence of Intrafamilial and Extrafamilial Sexual Abuse of Female Children," *Child Abuse and Neglect: The International Journal,* October, 1982.
2. David Finkelhor, *Sexual Victimization of Children* (New York: Free Press, 1979).
3. Dr. Robert Tenn-Bensel, as quoted in "Evangelism, Patriarch, and Abusive Children," by Virginia Mollenkott, *Radix Magazine,* January–February, 1982, Vol. 13, No. 4.
4. Jennifer James, Principal Investigator, "Entrance into Juvenile Prostitution," August, 1980; and "Entrance into Juvenile Male Prostitution," August, 1982.
5. Juvenile Sex Offender Program, University of Washington, Seattle, WA.
6. Marie Fortune, *Sexual Abuse Prevention: A Study for Teenagers* (New York: United Church Press, 1984), p. 9.
7. Fortune, op. cit., p. 9.

Session 3

1. Joy Wilt, *Mine and Yours* (Waco, TX: Educational Products), p. 122.
2. Wilt, op. cit., pp. 124–26.
3. Wilt, op. cit., p. 122.
4. Wilt, op. cit., pp. 124–26.

Session 4

1. Carol A. Plummer, *Preventing Sexual Abuse: Activities and Strategies for Those Working with Children and Adolescents* (Holmes Beach, FL: Learning Publications, Inc., 1984).

Session 5

1. The *lack of touch* concept is largely derived from the work of James Prescott, Ph.D., who has studied the effects of somatosensory deprivation. Dr. Prescott's studies indicate that children who receive physical affection during their formative years tend to inhibit later violence. ("Body Pleasure and the Orgins of Violence," *The Futurist,* April, 1975).
2. The Touch Continuum © 1979, reprinted with permission of Cordelia Anderson. Excerpts from the *Child Sexual Abuse Prevention Project Guidebook,* by Cordelia Anderson (Kent) Sexual Assault Services—Hennepin County Attorney's Office, Minneapolis, MN, 1979.
3. Fortune, op. cit., p. 22.
4. Fortune, op. cit., p. 22.
5. Fortune, op. cit., p. 23.

Session 7

1. Fortune, op. cit., p. 27.

2. Fortune, op. cit., p. 27.
3. Fortune, op. cit., p. 27.

Session 9

1. Plummer, op. cit., p. 71.

Session 11

1. Fortune, op. cit., p. 28.
2. Fortune, op. cit., p. 30.

Session 12

1. Fortune, op. cit., p. 30.
2. Fortune, op. cit., p. 31.
3. Fortune, op. cit., p. 31.
4. Fortune, op. cit., p. 31.

Appendix A

1. Plummer, op. cit., p. 145.

Appendix B

1. Mary Nelson and Kay Clark, eds., *Educator's Guide to Preventing Child Sexual Abuse* (Santa Cruz, CA: Network Publications, 1986), p. 182.

Appendix D

1. Adapted from Plummer, op. cit., p. 157–58.

Appendix E

1. Plummer, op. cit., p. 159.

Appendix F

1. Religious leaders should familiarize themselves with the child protective services office in their community. Some child protection programs do only investigation of possible abuse; others do both investigation and treatment. Ask about the specifics of the agency staff's approach to reports and the possible options available to them. Approach them as a professional ally and resource. Invite them to a discussion with local ministerial groups.
2. See Seward Reese, 1963, "Confidential Communications to Clergy," *Ohio State Law Journal,* 24:55.
3. *The Book of Discipline of the United Methodist Church,* 1980 (Nashville, TN: United Methodist Publishing House), 220, paragraph 440.4.
4. *The Minutes of the United Lutheran Church in America,* the 22nd Biennial Convention, 1960, as quoted in Reese, op. cit., p. 69.